Brilliant ideas

Learn everything there is to know about your home before you begin your design and decoration.

Settle on your style to create a room that's pleasing to the eye.

Find the shades and tones that suit your home. The pick 'n' mix approach is all very well at the cinema sweetie counter but...

Seen first and frequently passed through, your hallway deserves more attention than you may think.

Sand and stone, woodlands and heather strewn hillsides...nature provides inspiration for stunning interiors.

Take the plunge for a luxury bathroom. The most stimulating experience I have ever had naked was in a hotel in Las Vegas. And if you've never tried out a wet sauna, I can't recommend it highly enough.

Brilliant features

Each chapter of this book is designed to provide you with an inspirational idea that you can read quickly and put into practice straight away.

Throughout you'll find four features that will help you to get right to the heart of the idea:

- *Try another idea* If this idea looks like a life-changer then there's no time to lose. *Try another idea* will point you straight to a related tip to expand and enhance the first.

- *Here's an idea for you* Give it a go – right here, right now – and get an idea of how well you're doing so far.

- *Defining ideas* Words of wisdom from masters and mistresses of the art, plus some interesting hangers-on.

- *How did it go?* If at first you do succeed try to hide your amazement. If, on the other hand, you don't this is where you'll find a Q and A that highlights common problems and how to get over them.

Introduction

Set aside all the practical reasons why you have a home – a roof over your head, a place to sleep, somewhere to eat, storage for all your possessions – and consider just one thing:
do you love being there?

Does the combination of colours, the choice of furniture, the use of materials and the way it's been laid out fit perfectly with your tastes and lifestyle?

If you find yourself thinking that this is not entirely the case, then maybe it's time to make some changes. Here's where this book steps in.

There are guidelines that you can follow and advice that makes great sense and while I am not a fan of rules, some can be applied to tackling the design of your home (but don't feel that you always have to stick to them rigidly). Interpret them in your own way and for your specific situation.

You can seek the advice of a professional interior designer and they will do a magnificent job on decorating your home. But wouldn't it be more fun and give you greater satisfaction if you knew that the inspiration and execution were all your own?

This book will help you make the best decisions in design terms about every room. You may agree with some of the ideas and you may find others just don't fit with

your own perception of what makes a house a home. This has been written from one person's understanding and experience in choosing and using colours, fabrics, furniture and the space in which they will sit. It sets out to inspire rather than lay down the law, so please use it as a guide and not a set of rules.

It sets out to inform and instruct you how to approach certain activities and will hopefully result in you understanding much more about the space in which you live.

It's intended to be enjoyable. Designing and decorating may be hard work but it should be a labour of love. I hope this book helps you to create your perfect space be it the bedroom, bathroom, kitchen, lounge or hallway.

1

Home sweet home

Learn everything there is to know about your home before you begin your design and decoration.

There's a saying 'to know me is to love me', and in the case of my home it's a love that's grown over time. Getting used to a sloping floor and living with uneven walls seemed at first a little annoying, but now I love the charm of my slightly unusual rooms.

I've come to accept, for example, that there is no way that I can open up the chimney without incurring excessive costs. But I can still make a feature of it with a shelf above to simulate a mantelpiece and a pile of lovely logs to decorate the hearth. It's an illusion but it generates a cosy mood – even without the flames. Let's be honest. When we buy a property we rarely give it a thorough going over. Well, it's a bit embarrassing to get caught out with the spirit level by the owner of the house. And you are not going to be able to open every window, close every internal door, look at the construction of every cupboard (to see if the hideous DIY job can be ripped out), run every tap and move furniture around (to get a better idea of how to use the space) even during a second viewing.

Here's an idea for you...

Walk around the rooms in your new home. Look at where light fittings are positioned – both ceiling and wall mounted – as this will affect where you position your lamps. Measure up recesses because a piece of storage that was in your old dining room may fit perfectly in the lounge. Consider the flooring. With nothing cluttering up a room is there a spot where you would love to put down a designer rug so that it is seen in the best light? Why not position the furniture around it rather than vice versa, which is more usually the case? Is there a wall space that would be the perfect place for a piece of art or a monumental mirror? You don't want to waste the area by putting a tall cupboard or bookcase there.

Defining idea...

'A man builds a fine house; and now he has a master, and a task for life: he is to furnish, watch, show it, and keep it in repair, the rest of his days.'
RALPH WALDO EMERSON

Which means that the day you move in is a bit like going out on a date arranged by a dating agency. You've seen the picture of the person (house). You've read the biography of the individual concerned (estate agent's details). And you've realised you have no idea what you are going to do next because you don't know their preferences for food, their taste in film or their political leanings.

In 'house' terms these queries could translate into any of the following:

- Does the heating system really warm every room or will you have to redecorate in colours that will help raise the temperature in specific spaces?

- Will your minimalist interior preferences realistically work in a Victorian conversion or are you going to have to rethink your ideas to cope with small rooms rather than loft-style expanses?

- How much natural light does each room enjoy through the day and through the seasons, and are you going to have to invest in task lighting for a study or wall lamps for a living room in order to be able to use the space efficiently?

So how do you proceed in getting to know your home?

I would urge you initially to leave the unpacking (apart from kettle, teabags and mugs) and to go through the house with a large notepad and make notes. Do this before you empty all the boxes and clutter up the space. And if it means that you sleep on your mattress on the floor that night, then so be it. You may think this is unrealistic given the pressures of co-ordinating moving out and in with your purchasers and your vendor but at the very least give yourself an hour or two in the empty property. This is a time that you and the house will never have again because once the furniture is in place and you've put out your collection of china, the room has already been given a 'look'.

Consider these three things:

- **Light:** If you are going to need to maximise the light in a room but need privacy maybe you need to forget curtains but put in blinds that roll from the bottom of the window up rather than vice versa. Or choose designs that have a filtered panel as part of their make-up.

- **Colour:** Redecorating may be the last thing on your mind but could painting just one wall white in a green room make it seem bigger?

You can get the best use of any space by planning the layout of the room. See IDEA 34, *That hits the spot*, for more ideas.

Try another idea...

'*I have always felt that one of the greatest compliments anyone visiting your home can pay you is to sit down and take off their jacket unprompted, to be as easy and comfortable in your surroundings as you are. Although serendipity may come into it, such ease isn't accidental: on the contrary, comfort, simplicity, pleasure and practicality are the natural by-products of good design, a combination of intelligent planning, informed choice and creative application.*'
SIR TERENCE CONRAN

Defining idea...

3

■ **Balance:** Positioning furniture can create a formal, structured look to the room if everything is aligned, or a more casual relaxed look if pieces are set at angles or left 'floating' in open spaces.

By getting to know your space you'll have a much better chance of a creating a happy and harmonious home.

How did it go?

Q **I've considered all this careful planning but I know that by the time I get into the house, I will have to get the kids settled and two bedrooms and the lounge will need to be unpacked so they can at least watch TV while I tackle the rest of the house.**

A *Be prepared to be flexible. For starters, ask your agent before moving in if pictures were taken of every room, or if the owner will let you go in and do this. That way you can at least begin to work with existing colour schemes. Decide which rooms are a priority and leave them empty. Stack as many boxes as possible in the guest room so that you can plan the main bedroom, or load up the lounge but leave the kitchen clear for example.*

Q **OK, but there's only so much time that I can survive without the essentials for everyday living.**

A *Now this is a real pain but I have to advise you to plan your packing. It's so easy just to go round the rooms and pack everything available in the least time possible. I would advise you to assess each room before you start packing and label a box 'Essentials' for things that you know you won't be able to live without. You can put all of these boxes in one place when you arrive in your new home, so that at least you can access the more important things that you need.*

2

You've got the look

Settle on your style to create a room that's pleasing to the eye.

There is no way that you could or even should stick to every single rigid design rule when putting together your home. However, if you're happy to work with some guidelines in place, you'll reap the rewards in terms of creating an appealing and desirable space.

It's all about putting together the furniture, soft furnishings and accessories that match a certain mood.

I'm a minimalist, modernist, neutral colours kind of person and that means I have certain requirements in setting my style. There has to be plenty of storage in a room to keep it free from clutter. (I have serious storage issues but I do try to keep them behind closed doors.) The window treatments have to be simple. I have never contemplated curtains at any of my windows – it's always Roman blinds because of their clean lines. Fabrics are, in the main, natural: linen, wool, cotton and canvas. My vases are plain, clear glass and my flowers arrangements are always uncomplicated. And that's how to set a style.

Here's an idea for you...

Sit down and make a list of all the elements that you need. Break it down into the following: furniture, soft furnishings, flooring, window treatments, lighting and accessories. Now estimate a price beside each item on your list. It doesn't have to be exact, just a ballpark figure. Total this up and consider whether you can spend more or need to cut back. You can take away a chair and save some money or add an elaborate chandelier if you have the cash. Once you have a list that matches your budget, go to work on that room.

Think about spaces that you are drawn to. These could be a good indication of your personal style. (I loved the old Saatchi gallery in London's Westbourne Grove because it was just a vast, open, clutter-free space.) If you find yourself drawn to grand stately homes or always book a cosy country cottage for your holidays, these could be a starting point for tailoring a room to suit. Use a mood board to help you put together the look, incorporating a picture of your ideal room to inspire you as you work.

SO WHAT ELSE INFLUENCES YOUR STYLE?

Taste in music? You might worship at the feet of Elvis and so employ a retro approach to your interior.

Love of gardening? Cultivate a collection of floral prints that will give a theme for your scheme.

An historical period? Look for reproduction – or if you have the bank balance original – antique furniture.

Defining idea...

'To me style is just the outside of content, and content the inside of style, like the outside and inside of the human body – both go together, they can't be separated.'
JEAN-LUC GODARD

Another country? Source sumptuous silks from the Orient, porcelain painted in China or hand-carved accessories from Indonesia.

This should be polarising your thoughts. So now consider the practicalities of putting your plan into action.

Give yourself a budget: some looks are less expensive to achieve than others. What about structural alterations? Will knocking two rooms into one give you the space you need to make a dramatic statement? You might also give some thought to the future. If you are planning to stay in the house for only a couple of years, should you tone down the colour scheme so that you won't have to redecorate when you want to sell? Last but not least, will your style work in the space that you have? Light-drenched loft style is difficult to achieve in a basement flat.

If you set a style and get all the elements right, then you'll be happy to live with the look for years.

Here's an idea for you...

It's the lavish use of fabrics and ornate detailing that set a stately home style. Think long draping curtains complete with decorative pelmets and tasselled tiebacks. In the lounge you can look for a sofa that includes piles of cushions in its design. For the bedroom choose a four-poster bed or a design with a scrolling iron headboard and decorative posts finished with balls or finials. If you are drawn to this kind of place you'll be happy to fill the room with lots of extra furniture and accessories. Bring in a pouffe or covered footstool, a nest of tables and a writing desk complete with matching chair. Include one or two rugs on the floor to augment the 'soft' look of the room.

Try another idea...

If you are thinking about changing the lighting in one or two rooms, see IDEA 19, *An illuminating experience*, for some helpful hints.

Q   **I've designed my dining room around my love of English country gardens. I have used floral prints on the walls and a petal patterned fabric at the window, and put down some rugs with rose designs woven into the borders. We entertain regularly so there are always flowers on the table. During the summer there is a lot of natural light and I'm quite happy with the busy design, but how can I lighten it up a bit in the winter months?**

A   *It sounds like you have embraced the principles of planning a look, but it's also good to give rooms a mini facelift from time to time. Try the following. Take down one of the floral prints and replace it with a mirror. A gold frame might be a good choice to add a little touch of glitz. Have some slip covers made for the dining chairs in plain white cotton – this will lighten the room. Do you have a pendant light or wall lights? You may want to change the shades to a lighter fabric or even glass designs. Take the rugs away and see if that alters the mood. It might be a good opportunity to have them professionally cleaned and you can view the room without them.*

Q   **I have realised that the different items that I own suit a whole different range of styles. I don't want to get rid of some pieces. What do I do?**

A   *There are certain key items that do set a style. The sofa in the lounge and the bed in the bedroom would be two such pieces. Now it would be silly to suggest that everything that isn't modern, antique, blue or green, depending on your scheme, should be dumped. Remember that you're creating a home, not a museum or a show house, and allow yourself a few pieces in any space that are there just because you like them rather than because they are a perfect fit. That's part of what makes a house a home.*

3

Work that colour

Find the shades and tones that suit your home. The pick 'n' mix approach is all very well at the cinema sweetie counter but. . .

Colour scheming your whole house may sound like a huge challenge but by breaking it down room by room it is simply a matter of application. And in order to create a harmonious environment, it's really the only sensible approach.

OH GOOD GRIEF, DO I HAVE TO BE SENSIBLE?

Well yes, if you want to end up without colour clashes and disharmony as you move from room to room. Imagine when all the doors in the house are open being able to see a little bit of purple to the left (lounge), some green to the right (dining room), and walking through yellow (hallway), as you head for the blue kitchen. It's a quite a prospect isn't it?

(On a very practical level, if your room colours complement each other, then furniture, furnishings and accessories should work in a number of different places.

Here's an idea for you...

You may already have a room that is wallpapered and it can be fag or just a downright waste of time to strip the room in order to match your overall scheme. Choose a colour from the paper, it may be a touch of blue in the print, for example, and then use that in an adjacent room to link the two together.

This means that you can move pieces around your home when you want a change of scene, or to swap dining room for living room or guest room for master bedroom for example.)

I'm not the colour police. This approach doesn't mean that you have to be all white at every turn (apart from woodwork on which I would very rarely use any other paint). My advice is to stick with colours from the same broad family spectrum across most of your home or at least introduce the same colour in some form or another in each room. But there are three alternatives for successful colour scheming so take your pick from the list below. And if you decide to break the law in the odd space (hopefully just the box room) then you can live with your own guilt.

Take a look at a colour wheel and consider adopting the red and orangey siblings. Move around the wheel and introduce yourself to the yellow and greens or opt for the blues and purples. Each of these groups can affect your mood and effect changes of perception of the shape and size of the room. At the most basic level, for example, a red dining room will stimulate, a yellow dining room will cheer you up, and a blue room will engender a sense of calm.

The size of rooms should have an influence on your colour choices. If you have a series of small rooms you'll need to stick to a lighter palette. Where there's the luxury of generous proportions you can afford to move to the darker colours in the spectrum.

Here are your choices:

- **A tonal scheme:** This is where you pick just one colour but use it in varying tones. With purples, for example, you might combine the palest lavender and lilac, magenta, plum and wine. For greens, you might use eau de nil, olive, sage and pine.

- **A harmonious scheme:** Choose colours that are closely associated. The best way to do this is to look at a rack of paint charts and take three or four adjacent to each other. Start with red, next to it you'll find terracotta, copper and then chestnut.

- **A complementary scheme:** This uses colours that are opposites of each other. Orange versus blue, green versus purple, yellow versus scarlet. You will need to decide which one of the two colours will be more dominant in a room; indecision here can cause infighting that will wreck the scheme.

Whichever of the above you choose, one simple way to unify the rooms in a house is to stick with the same colour for your woodwork throughout.

YOU MAY HAVE HEARD THIS A THOUSAND TIMES BUT LISTEN AGAIN!

Start out by buying tester pots. Then paint large pieces of white paper in your chosen colours and pin them up around your home. Leave them for several days. Watch how the light affects them in different rooms and swap them around to see how they may

Try another idea...

If you like the idea of using neutral and natural colours for your scheme see IDEA 5, **Natural stimulation**. For an all-white approach, turn to IDEA 11, **When white is right**.

Defining idea...

'*Colour possesses me. I don't have to pursue it. It will possess me always, I know it.*'
PAUL KLEE

alter the perspective of a space. Make notes. Let someone else have an opinion (within reason). But do not paint a wall until you have lived with them for a least a week.

'Fools rush in' when it comes to making colour choices, so take time and take care and you won't 'fear to tread' in any of your rooms.

How did it go?

Q I've used a complementary scheme of lilac and green in the dining room but the purple on every wall seems to dominate the room.

A *You can create balance by including a neutral colour in the space. A grey will work with green and purple. Use the tester pot experiment and paint a piece of paper in a soft grey. Something subtle like mink. Stick it on one or two walls at different times of the day to see which best helps it balance the scheme. For other complementary schemes, a taupe will work with both blue and orange, and white is just right for yellow and scarlet.*

Q OK, but what if I can't face repainting a wall?

A *This is where you can use furniture, flowers and accessories – basically any tool in the designer's repertoire to make it work. Position a set of shelves in a neutral colour against one of the main walls to break up the expanse of purple. Or find a print or picture that you can hang on one wall that, again, will break up the block of colour. A huge bunch of beautiful white lilies placed in the middle of a table will always draw the eye to that particular spot.*

4

Welcome to my world

Seen first and frequently passed through, your hallway deserves more attention than you may think.

There are certain spaces that we often neglect. It is lack of thought more than a deliberate disregard, and the hall all too often falls into this list. In fact it could well be at the top.

Which is ludicrous when you think that this is the first space that you see when you get home and the last area that you pass through when you leave. Think about all the trips that you make through this space. You probably go through it in the morning to get tea from the kitchen and then you traverse it again on your way back upstairs to have a shower. Later on, you retrace your steps downstairs to make breakfast and then you nip into the hall to pick up the post. Are you getting the idea? You spend more time in the hall than you think. So it should, above all other rooms, deserve careful attention and a loving touch.

- **Make it welcoming:** A chair or reclaimed church pew that is tucked against the wall allows people to rest for a minute after they walk through the door.

Here's an idea for you... **A decorative chimney pot or length of earthenware pipe, placed in a stylish bowl, makes an alternative umbrella stand.**

- **Keep it useful:** Coat hooks, umbrella stands, a mat to wipe feet on and a table to dump the post on make it a functional space

- **Light it right:** Make sure that you have switches at the bottom and top of the staircase. If it's very dark, consider replacing a solid wood front door with a design that has glass panels.

- **Make your home secure:** Add as many devices as you want: bolts, chains and a spy hole are all advisable.

It's more than likely that this area leads into other spaces so choose a colour scheme that won't clash with adjacent rooms. It is also probable that there is a lot of empty wall space and you could easily use it to hang a collection of prints. Are there areas that you could use to create extra storage space or redefine for another purpose? The space under the stairs, for example, might be used to house a desk or utilised as a laundry. These are all details that will enhance the look and functionality of your hall.

STEP BY STEP

Give plenty of thought to your staircase. What seems to be an immovable feature can be replaced or dressed up according to your budget. Accepting that wood is the material that most of us will inherit when we move into our home, it's a revelation when you think about the other materials that can be used to construct a staircase: glass, concrete and steel are all utilised in new builds and conversions to fit in with the overall scheme of an interior.

Consider one of the following options:

- If you need to bring more light into the space, then choose a glass balustrade and beechwood treads.

- Should you want to continue an open plan theme, commission a hanging wire system where the treads are seemingly suspended in space.

- Do you live in an industrial-style loft? Add rubber treads to the edge of each step.

- Want to be decorative but can't afford a runner (and they can be pricey)? Then leave the central half of each step in natural wood and paint the quarter each side to match the balustrade.

- Modernising an old building? Cover the steps with flexible zinc sheeting.

If you take the time to pay attention to your hallway you'll be rewarded with a welcome every time.

'I have heard that stiff people lose something of their awkwardness under high ceilings, and in spacious halls.'
RALPH WALDO EMERSON

Defining idea...

There are plenty of options when you come to choose the flooring for your hall. IDEA 28, *A tough decision*, may give you some ideas.

Try another idea...

'There is room in the halls of pleasure
For a large and lordly train,
But one by one we must all file on
Through the narrow aisles of pain.'
ELLA WHEELER WILCOX,
American poet

Defining idea...

How did it go?

Q **I realise that I've neglected the staircase and I'm thinking about painting the wood so that it matches the walls. What do you think?**

A *In theory this sounds lovely. But can I just tell you that there is no worse job in the decorating arena than painting or stripping the spindles, so unless you can pay someone to do the job, you might want to consider living with what you have. I know from experience the pain, anguish, tears and monumental boredom that are involved in tackling this job. My observation is that you have to be having the love affair of your life – the one – the only – the 'never felt like this before and don't believe I ever will again' relationship with your home if you are prepared to go through this.*

If you still want to go ahead, then make sure you prepare the woodwork for paint, set aside a month of Sundays and good luck to you.

Q **I have a dark hallway so I chose a light-coloured carpet for the flooring, however, it's now getting very grubby, particularly by the front door. If I put a mat down it's going to obstruct the doorway, so what should I do?**

A *Make yourself a mat well. Measure up an area roughly 1 metre long from the door and remove the carpet using a heavy-duty craft knife. Take this along to a carpet specialist and find a coir or seagrass that is of the same thickness as your carpet. Order a mat to be made up to the dimensions of the space that you have cut and drop it into place. Fix a threshold strip between the two types of flooring to neaten the join.*

5

Natural stimulation

**Sand and stone, woodlands and heather strewn hillsides...
nature provides inspiration for stunning interiors.**

Whether you choose whitewashed walls
reminiscent of crumbling cliffs or a smoky
grey grass flooring that reminds you of walks on
the moors, there is endless stimulation for the
jaded designer when you look outside.

Using natural materials in a room makes for a relaxed and comfortable space. And
small pieces from the great outdoors – a rough length of driftwood in the
bathroom, a vase of smooth pebbles in the lounge, a bowl of sea-worn iridescent
seashells beside the bed – all offer a way of introducing interesting texture into
your home.

I like to sit down and list the looks and finishes I want to mimic when creating a
naturally inspired interior:

- The roughened texture of yellowy grass on a sand dune

- The silvery brown of a worn tree trunk

Here's an
idea for
you...

The most fun you can have with furniture is to copy a technique that I saw, and got to try out, on a visit to a fine furniture factory. The company specialised in repro pieces and part of the process of turning new into old involved repeatedly beating a cabinet. The tool used was a collection of nuts and bolts (I added a couple of keys when I did this at home) on a chain. Repeatedly flog the surface until you have knicks, scratches and dents to suit. It's fine therapy too.

- The fluffy, curly, creamy wool from a sheep

- The myriad of smooth greys on pebbles by the shores of a lake

Whether your closest outdoor escape is a forest, a field or a beach, use that environment as a starting point for planning a room. (If you feel it's time for a break, take a walk in the country now! Take snapshots of the things you see as you stroll with your fabulous mobile phone or digital camera and you can download these images and use them in your mood board for the room.)

All these colours are in some way slightly bleached out. They are subtle and no one shade stands out as dominant. This means you can mix and match them to your heart's content without creating colour clashes in a space.

Imagine a grey flannel-covered sofa or chair, a mellow seagrass flooring, a chunky beechwood table. Put these in the midst of a room where the backdrop is a limestone-coloured wall and the windows are draped with unbleached linen curtains and you are beginning to commune with nature.

There's one collection of paints you must look at: Kelly Hoppen's Perfect Neutrals from Fired Earth. Choose from Shell, Bone, Pebble, Linen, Orchid, Tusk, Clotted Cream, etc., etc., etc. – all gloriously evocative names (though how you visualise In

Love With Taupe without seeing it bears some thought). These are colours that you'll come back to time and time again. You'll reuse them when you move from one home to the next because they are just perfect examples of the best of the natural palette.

But aren't they a bit bland? I here the colour cravers cry . . .

'Nature does nothing in vain.'
ARISTOTLE

Defining idea...

If you like the idea of natural flooring take a look at IDEA 41, *The soft side*, for some materials that might suit.

Try another idea...

Here's where you rely on texture to bring that interest into the space. I love natural fibre for floors. There's something refreshing about the thought that you are walking on grass (yes a refined type I know). But if that option is a little bit too rough for your tastes (and I would avoid it in bedrooms), then I would suggest a loop pile carpet. In flecked wool this is both practical and pretty much perfect for a natural scheme. And you'll see the texture.

Next fabrics. No smooth silks or flat cottons. For blinds, use hessian and wicker weaves. For curtains choose one of the 'new' suedes. They look like the real thing but are a fraction of the cost. You are looking for anything that has a 'touchy-feely' quality, so a rough linen or a robust corduroy also fit the bill. Knitted cushion covers or throws with bobbles and fringes are just what you need.

If you let a love of nature inspire your interiors you'll find it easy to create a mellow and relaxing home.

'The unreal is natural, so natural that it makes of unreality the most natural of anything natural.'
GERTRUDE STEIN

Defining idea...

How did it go?

Q   I understand the point of introducing texture but all my walls are new plaster, so beautifully smooth, and my furniture is mostly pine.

A   *The quickest solution is to think about using paint effects. (No, I'm not going to begin a lesson in stencilling so don't turn the page just yet.) You can use them for maximum impact with a natural colour palette. Texturing, ageing or crackle-glazing are perfect for these rooms. You can add sand to emulsion to give walls a subtle grain, or layer a base coat onto a piece of furniture, rub over the surface with a candle and then add a topcoat in a slightly lighter shade of the base colour. Sand the whole piece and the paint comes away from the waxed areas giving you the textured appearance of years of wear and tear.*

Q   I've used coir in the room but now I've come to clean, how do I treat the flooring?

A   *If it wasn't supplied with a stain inhibitor then you must get the flooring treated as you need to protect against any liquid spillages. You shouldn't use water or shampoo on these natural floorings as they will absorb the moisture and expand or wrinkle. If something gets knocked over, soak it up instantly. Allow mud or dirt to dry out before tackling it. Simply brush the area to loosen the mud and then give the room a vacuum. Use furniture cups under chair legs or castors, as this type of flooring will mark.*

6

Wet, wet, wet rooms

Take the plunge for a luxury bathroom. The most stimulating experience I have ever had naked was in a hotel in Las Vegas. And if you've never tried out a wet sauna, I can't recommend it highly enough.

In the middle of The Pink Flamingo spa (even though 'Bugsy' Siegel's original Flamingo is now gone, the hotel that still carries the name is no less glamorous) you can sit until it's hot enough to fry an egg on your leg and then pull a chain and get deluged with freezing water.

Once you can breathe again – roughly 20 seconds later – you do the same thing all over again and again and again. This is the perfect way to wash away the memory of losses at the blackjack table and effective as a hangover cure for the free Jack Daniels at the roulette wheel. (But is not recommended for anyone too highly strung or with any kind of heart condition – but then they probably wouldn't be in Vegas anyway.)

Here's an idea for you...

For the ultimate in luxury include a television in the room: you won't have to miss a moment of a movie or the start of the football. The latest version looks like a tinted mirror until you switch it on (using your credit card sized remote control) and it has a heated screen so that you'll still be able to see the picture however hot and steamy it gets in the room.

A word of caution: *be very careful* when researching wet rooms on the web. Start by going for upmarket bathroom specialists and tile companies to get professional advice. Even on Google, the websites that come up when using 'wet rooms' as a search term include a diverse cross-section of porn available on the net.

When I got home from my trip, I began to research the idea of having some kind of spa at home...and quickly realised that I'd have to go back to the States in order to win enough money to pay for a wet room. But don't let that put you off. You can simplify things and include elements such as a whirlpool bath or a large enough for two walk-in shower cubicle into your bathroom without breaking the bank. You can invest in a specially designed shower cubicle with a gently sloping floor that allows excess water to be contained in a small area. Team that with glass walls for the cubicle and you can kid the pickiest bather that there's a freestanding shower in the room.

If you want to go the whole hog and include a shower without a screen, a 'barrier-free' bathroom where water runs into a well in a gently sloping floor, the most important consideration is to find a builder – or bathroom designer – with experience of wet rooms. The floor may need to be raised to allow for a slope and in older houses the floor may not support the weight of a new stone or fully tiled floor. It isn't just a question of retiling, the surfaces will need to be lined and sealed, which is a specialist job. At this point it is also worth thinking about underfloor heating. I would always recommend installing it as the room will be much more inviting in the winter months. You might also want to consider a sunken tub. Consult with your builder or designer to see if it will fit in with the raising of the floor and can be fitted into a recessed area.

If you want to think about the space before you commit to a wet room, turn to IDEA 17, Bathe in style.

Try another idea...

When you are considering sanitary ware and furniture, go for wall-mounted pieces in every situation possible.

LAP OF LUXURY

Super showers now offer such a range of luxury facilities you can easily recreate the spa experience at home. In contrast to the classic over-the-bath dribbling handset, you want a heavy-duty spray.

The importance of a powerful shower cannot be emphasised enough. Showers need sufficient water pressure to maintain a steady flow so the position of your water tank could affect the installation. *Again, this is why you must have an experienced designer or builder on the job.*

**'What would the world be, once bereft
Of wet and wildness?
Let them be left,
O let them be left,
wildness and wet,
Long live the weeds and the
wildness yet.'**
GERARD MANLEY HOPKINS

Defining idea...

23

Defining
idea...

'Some men are like musical glasses; to produce their finest tones you must keep them wet.'
SAMUEL TAYLOR COLERIDGE

When choosing your fixtures look out for a steam version that incorporates an overhead shower, lighting and maybe speakers that can be built into the ceiling. (No point in scrimping on the luxury element if you are doing this properly, and tunes in the steam room are a plus.) Shower designers know that if you are going to steam you need to really relax, so some have thoughtfully added seats to their products. Include a shower design that offers adjustable jets or side sprays so that you can massage whichever bit of cellulite is bothering you that day. After you've steamed you'll want to cool off with a deluge of cold water, so look for an appropriately named flood shower that recreates a waterfall effect overhead. Sound like a lot of fixtures? Well modern technology means that you can find all these features in a single model.

FINISHING TOUCHES

Natural materials suit the style of a wet room. Marble, granite, slate, wood and glass should all be considered in the materials that you choose. Small mosaic tiles on the walls will give the room a Mediterranean feel; duck boarding sets a Scandinavian mood. If you want to add a wall to divide any area of the room – to prevent the basin or loo from getting splashed every time you enjoy a vigorous session in the shower for example – create a panel from glass bricks for a modern look.

The beauty of a spa-type bathroom is that it functions as somewhere to get clean, somewhere to relax and somewhere to indulge yourself. If you are a bit of a water baby, it's the perfect room.

Q **The idea of waterproofing the whole room sounds a bit extreme. I live in an old house and it sounds like a lot of work. Can you tell me more?**

How did it go?

A *Yes it does involve a lot of work, especially if you have a suspended wooden floor which will have to be raised to accommodate the drain. It needs to be waterproofed as this is the only way that you can set up the space so that it doesn't matter where the water flows and which surfaces it hits. Professionals also describe it as 'tanking' the room. More often than not this involves taking up the existing wooden floor. You then angle it to the waste and drain and cover the whole thing with a material such as ply or fibreglass. Finally a rubberised solution can be used to seal the whole surface.*

Q **So if I do have this done is there any point in me putting in a shower screen?**

A *No, that's the whole point. It won't matter where the water from the shower goes. The only reason you might have for using one is if you want to protect the loo or bath from getting a drenching every time you take a shower, but if you position them on the opposite side of the room to the shower head you shouldn't have a problem.*

7

Curtain call

Frame your windows and let the fabric do the work. When you smarten up your sashes or bring colour to your casements, you are complementing a colour scheme or fitting in with a particular look.

Do you want casual drapes running on curtain rings and a pole or are you looking for a more formal treatment where the curtains are teamed up with a pelmet and dressy tiebacks?

Your choice of curtains should reflect the mood of the room. Keep it simple if you are living in a modern environment, a neat pencil pleat heading and plain pole for example, and go OTT if you have a classic look in mind, and I mean indulge your windows with pelmets, tiebacks and tasselled trimmings.

There is a plethora of different looks for your curtains but you should always be generous with the fabric that you use. Whatever the style of the room, the curtains should comfortably cover the window; if the fabric has to be pulled quite flat to meet in the middle they will always look cheap, cheap, cheap. Allow a minimum of two times the width of the window and a maximum of three when you buy it. (You can go for more but it is only necessary for the most opulent of designs.)

Here's an idea for you...

If you have a room that isn't overlooked, consider leaving your windows bare of any traditional treatment. With any kind of view outside this creates an amazing impact when people walk into the room. If it seems a bit bare, pick a mixture of vases of different heights. Arrange the same kind of flowers in each receptacle and place in front of one or two panes, keeping the tallest to the side panes of the run of windows. Alternatively use the sills to display pictures or photographs, propped up against the glass and moved around on a regular basis to change the mood.

Those clever designs that seem effortlessly to pool on the floor can look amazing. This look works better with light fabric that flows and drapes easily; anything too heavy will bulk up on the floor into a heavy pile rather than sink down into a light pool.

FABRIC CHOICES

Never buy fabric for curtains based on a tiny swatch. You will have no idea about how a print will look when it is made up into curtains if you have only seen a small square of the design. It would be a bit like buying a still-life when the artist has only sketched a single apple: how are you going to know what the overall finished piece will look like? The best way to get an idea when you are buying fabric for this job is to grab the roll off the shelf in the shop and pull out a metre or two so that you can see the complete repeat of a design. No sales assistant in the soft furnishings department worth his or her salt will frown on you doing this and if they do, just stare them down. After all, if you are dressing two or three windows in the same room you might be investing a large amount of money.

Depending on the place that you are decorating, look to lovely shears, muslins and voiles for rooms where you want the light to flood in. They have a luxurious air when allowed to drape in generous swathes. One trick to add a more formal touch is to hang them behind a pelmet which is covered in a contrasting fabric. Choose damasks, heavy linen and textured silk when you want to make more of a statement with the drapes when they are closed. There is no doubt that you will have already made a decision about your colour scheme when you come to choose the fabric but think about the different effects that patterns can achieve. If you want to create the illusion of extra height, then opt for a design with a vertical stripe. If you want to add width, then pick a material with a horizontal design.

Just a note on poles. If your fabric is opulent, choose a suitably grand pole and make sure that the finials are dressy too. For sheer designs, keep the pole understated – something that ends with a simple curl would be fine.

Take the time to research your fabric choices and match the treatment to the mood of the room and you are on the right road for creating gorgeous windows.

The dining room is often a place for opulent window treatments. See IDEA 29, *Eating in is the new eating out*, for ways of designing this room.

Try another idea...

'Either those curtains go or I do.'
OSCAR WILDE

Defining idea...

'It is god in the house when the curtains lift gently at the windows.'
ELLEASE SOUTHERLAND,
African-American author

Defining idea...

29

How did it go?

Q I have chosen a patterned fabric for my curtains but it's quite sheer so they will need lining. What type of fabric do you suggest I use?

A *Have you ever thought about combining different fabrics? A pattern lined with a stripe looks quite special when you can see a little of the stripe when the curtains are pulled back. Use a tieback to make sure you can create this look. You'll need to manipulate the fabric a little so that the stripes show. If you then use some of the same material to make up a couple of cushion covers it ties a scheme together beautifully.*

Q I have a small window on one wall in the dining room – is there anything I can do to make it seem bigger?

A *It's easy to alter the proportions of a window by careful positioning of a pelmet and pole. If you fix your pelmet so that the bottom edge just barely covers the top of the window frame, no one will see just exactly where the window finishes. Allow your pole to extend each side to one-third of the width of a small window. When you draw the curtains allow the inside edge to just brush the sides of the frame. No one will be able to guess just how narrow the window really is. .*

8

Work that room

Get the best out of your home office. You are saving a ridiculous amount of time by not travelling to and from work each day when you set up an office at home. But if the environment isn't functional and your use of the space less than efficient, you may not reap the benefits.

In creating a work area at home you want it to be able to operate independently from the rest of the house.

Have you thought about converting a garden shed or garage into a work area? Or having a dedicated building installed in the garden that you can then make into an office? I have even read of an office being constructed in a tree house, so think laterally about where you have space that could be used (and just imagine how lovely it would to be stuck up a tree all day!).

If you aren't lucky enough to have a dedicated room, what are your office options? You need to create a space in another place and the dining room is a perfect spot for doubling up. There is already a table and chairs (although you should invest in a dedicated work chair – you are going to be sitting for several hours a day and don't want to end up with backache). You probably already have plenty of lamps and good dedicated lighting in the dining room and adding another piece of storage that won't look out of place shouldn't be too tricky if you pick a unit that matches your existing colour scheme.

Here's an idea for you...

If your office is situated in a dual-purpose room it's more than worth investing in a unit that will house your work area but can be closed off at the end of the day. Faux wardrobes or bookcases are widely available. If you work in the lounge, use leather suitcases or adapt blanket boxes as storage for files. In a guest room you can easily disguise the bed during work hours by positioning it against a wall and covering it with throws and a mix of cushions.

If you need to adopt a corner of the lounge, try and make sure that you position your desk on the same side of the room as the door and preferably behind where it opens into the space. That way, if you don't tidy up at the end of everyday, a cluttered desk isn't the first thing that people see when they walk into the room. I would urge you to invest in a screen. Whether you opt for a Japanese-style paper design, an old-fashioned fabric piece or even a wooden screen, this can be moved into place to disguise the work area and moved out of the way when you have nothing to hide.

Avoid working in the bedroom if you can. You need to get away from the office and if work is on your mind when you go to bed, and within easy reach, it's a recipe for an unsettled night.

I started out with a fairly chaotic approach to the 'office environment' when I started working from home but quickly realised that I needed to address a few specific issues.

- **Time is money:** Don't start doing all the jobs that you used to fit in at the weekend during your working day.

- **Good communication is a must:** Have a dedicated phone, fax and internet line for your work.

- **Organisation is essential:** Make sure that you have storage, then get some storage, and finally bring in some more storage. There is nothing more off-putting when you start the working day than piles of papers on the floor and a desk littered with literature.

- **Layout is key:** Set up the space so that information you need instant access to is positioned near to the desk. Occasional reference material can go in a cupboard on the other side of the room.

If you are put off by working in chaos, IDEA 15, *Keep it tidy*, may help you clear the decks.

Try another idea...

'The presence of a second building behind the main house made the property all the more attractive to Hemingway, because it was there that he could make his study a refuge, a place where he could create, and was accessible by way of an exterior flight of iron stairs. He lined the walls with shelving, filled them with books, and acquired a plain round table. Here he installed himself, sitting upon a leather-covered stick chair purchased from a cigar factory. The process began every day in the peace of the early morning and generally continued for a good six hours.'
FRANCESCA PREMOLI-DROULERS,
Writers' Houses

Defining idea...

- **Safety is an issue:** Keep an eye on the number of plugs going into sockets and extension leads and keep cabling organised so that it doesn't get into a spaghetti-like state.

- **Lighting must be right:** Get dedicated task lighting. Do position a lamp on your desk but don't allow it to reflect on the screen.

- **You need a good ambience:** I have an 'energising' scented candle to burn and keep flowers on my desk.

- **Avoid distractions:** Position your office away from the busy or family areas of the home.

- **Make it a dedicated space:** Try and keep the office area clear of anything that isn't related to your work.

If you try to implement as many of the above as possible, you should find working from home works for you.

Q I've been getting backache after working for several hours. I'm using an office-style chair that I bought second-hand but I do a lot of keying-in work and my back seems to be getting worse. What can I do?

How did it go?

A *It sounds to me like you need to chuck out the chair and go to a professional office supplies company. Explain the type (no pun intended) of work that you do, how long you are seated and take along a measurement of the height of your desk or table. You may need a chair with flexible height positioning for the seat so that your feet can sit flat on the ground when you work. Does the back support you when you sit forward to type and sit back to read? You should be looking for a design that supports your spine at all times.*

Q OK, but I'm still not comfortable for longer than an hour or so.

A *And why should you be? You must take regular breaks when working at a computer. My optician recommends that I move away from my desk and walk around every 10 or 15 minutes for general well-being as well as to protect my eyes. Get a cup of tea, open the post or grab a snack – but make sure that you are taking regular breaks.*

9

Choosing the blues

An ocean colour scene. From tranquil seas and stormy skies to classic tunes and Paul Newman's eyes, the blues can do no wrong.

In choosing blue and including blue, you bring a calming influence to your home. A place or space with a hint of blue is somewhere you'll find that you can relax. I'm not a hippy, but trust me (along with a raft of well-trained and very well-educated colour therapists): colours do affect your mood.

I am that sure whichever colour you are drawn to, blue or red or yellow or black or white, it is tied into memories both good and bad. Holidays, high days, hellos and goodbyes...in the same way that I have a record that reminds me of a certain time, so a colour is evocative. Blue reminds me of years at college beside the sea in Bournemouth. And a once in a lifetime holiday in Barbados, where the sea and sky is always blue and your mood is always good (rum hangovers aside).

Here's an idea for you...

You might find the seaside scheme from the Mediterranean too bright so try out a nautical look that owes more to the yachts and boats of the Isle of Wight. Think about a traditional nautical scene with deep navy heavy-duty cotton fabrics to cover sofas and chairs. Avoid a simple two-tone room and bring in a touch of deckchair stripe with a hint of pink or green for blinds or curtains, and small touches of sandy taupe in rugs or throws. Why not strip back floorboards to introduce a touch of wood or perhaps invest in a classic steamer chair where the combination of canvas upholstery and a wood frame encompass the look of the whole. Think ship's galley. Bring in pebble grey in the form of accessories, whether it's a stone vase or slate bowl, to complete the room.

SO WHY CHOOSE BLUES?

Well, they are calming and serene. They bring peace and tranquillity. They can be austere and they can be welcoming. Cool blues, with a grey or greeny shade, are cold. If you have a north-facing room where natural daylight is reduced to a watery trickle in the winter and a solitary sun-rising hour in the summer, it most certainly isn't an option for the lounge. But it may be perfect for a study or office, where concentration and focus are important. Warm blues that fall towards the purple part of the spectrum are perfect for halls and passageways. Let's think about some schemes.

In the Mediterranean and the Caribbean, bold and vivid blues reflect the colour of a sunny sky and warm sea. Teamed with a liberal use of white this combination is buoyant and bright. If you've had a holiday in such a location, they will bring back great memories and for that reason alone may be perfect for you to use. The bathroom, in particular, with bold blue mosaics as a backdrop for a classic white suite will always look fresh. The blues to choose are bright and vibrant, often shades of turquoise. When you use this palette you can afford to introduce a touch of zingy green. Bring in a lime green cushion cover or throw to add a point of interest in the room. Or pile up limes in a white bowl for a stylish display that complements the colour scheme. Look for chalky whites to work with your blues and find fabrics with their own texture, like linen and muslin.

When all is said and done blues are the ideal basis for well-designed modern and classic schemes.

'There is no blue without yellow and without orange.'
VINCENT VAN GOGH

Defining idea...

If you aren't sure about which fabrics to choose for your window treatments, have a look at IDEA 7, *Curtain call*, and IDEA 22, *Blind ambition*.

Try another idea...

'A powerful palette to my mind is a palette that's not just a set of interesting or strong colours: it's something that has it's own identity above those colours and which can trigger strong associations, sometimes in our subconscious, of a time, place or emotion. A single colour can of course trigger such associations by itself, like a Miles Davis solo can. The palette, on the other hand, can work like a full orchestra.'
KEVIN McCLOUD, *Choosing Colours*

Defining idea...

How did it go?

Q **I like the idea of a blue scheme but I have a home built over a century ago. Any tips for a scheme?**

A *For a more classic look, think about using a period palette. Heritage colours are available in most paint ranges and include shades that are particularly suited to a older homes. These colours are more restrained and can be used across panelled walls and to highlight architectural features. Consider using Wedgwood Blue with its wonderful history. Whites should be flat and matt. Stay away from anything with a shimmer or shine.*

Q **OK, that's the paint. What else should I team with it?**

A *One thing you can do is look to include some decorative prints at the windows in curtains or blinds. Toile de Jouy, which is available in a number of colours but looks particularly stunning in blue, features country scenes, people and plants in historical settings. Team this with a heavy cotton fabric with a slim blue stripe to cover sofas or chairs.*

10

The great outdoors

A well-designed balcony, patio or roof terrace is a joy. This isn't a gardening guide so don't look for planting advice.

However, if part of your property includes one or more of the above, these spaces deserve as much attention as the interior rooms of your home.

And that's how to look at them – as outdoor rooms. They can work year round too – you don't confine your use of the bathroom to two months in the summer and your kitchen works for you twelve months of the year, so why not an outdoor space? If you live in an urban environment you will relish your outdoor space even more, as a peaceful retreat from the city bustle.

LAYING THE GROUNDWORK

Deck the space. Don't mess around with other surfaces unless you already have flagstones, terracotta tiles or cobbles already in place. Timber decking is inexpensive, durable and good looking, and gets better looking with age as long as it is well maintained. (If only we could all lay claim to the above.) There are plenty of designs that you can fit yourself, but if you don't take the DIY approach it's not necessarily expensive to pay someone to fix a deck. Consider getting all the materials yourself rather than asking the fitter to supply them; that way you can shop around. If you

Here's an idea for you...

Over time the timber will repeatedly get wet and then dry out and you may see small splits appear in the decking. Any knots in the wood could also exude resin. These are part and parcel of the appeal of timber. Neither will cause any damage, but you can brush away resin with a stiff brush once it has dried, and apply a water-repellent coating or specialist decking treatment once a year that will protect the surface to a large degree.

plan well ahead and buy in winter for laying the following summer you can find real bargains, as garden centres change their stock seasonally.

Brush your deck regularly with a stiff broom and wash the surface down at least a couple of times a year with a specialist cleaner. If you can beg, borrow or be bothered to hire a high-pressure jet cleaner, all the better.

SAFETY FIRST

Unless your space is at ground level make sure that railings around the area are secure. *Really, really* secure. People do like to lean their backsides against a surface when they have a drink in one hand. I went one step further and had walls built on two sides of my roof terrace to give a little more privacy from the neighbours. This means I don't have to worry even when children go out there because it is totally secure. (Then the old school next door that had been empty for years got planning permission to be made into flats. Now I am overlooked whatever corner I choose to sit in, so no more topless sunbathing for me.)

DRESSING UP

Garden canopies – yes or no? To be frank, don't bother with the expense of made-to-measure designs. I think the cost of making and fitting them far outweighs the benefits, although you will find plenty of companies that will totally disagree with that. It's a judgement call. Instead, use parasols on stands (or beach brollies stuck in large terracotta pots filled with dirt or sand), which are far more flexible anyway. You can move them around the area according to the direction of the sun or to protect you from the prevailing winds.

Use solar-powered garden lights. I know intellectually that any qualified electrician can come around and install outdoor lighting with all the appropriate safety features, but emotionally the combination of rain and electricity still alarms me. I inherited outdoor lamps wired into the house. I won't change the bulbs unless I am wearing my rubber-soled trainers and washing-up gloves (yes they're rubber too). Alternatively, rely on candle flares. They're much more fun anyway and also generate a bit of warmth.

Should you cover the outdoor area? See IDEA 18, *People in glass houses...*, if you really want to use the space all year round.

Try another idea...

'If you have a garden and a library, you have everything you need.'
MARCUS TULLIUS CICERO

Defining idea...

'The best place to seek God is in a garden. You can dig for him there.'
GEORGE BERNARD SHAW

Defining idea...

Metal or wood furniture? (Don't even think about plastic.) This is a style call. If your outdoor space leads off a modern chrome-filled kitchen, choose a contemporary powder-coated steel or rustproof aluminium set that reflects the mood. Should you have patio doors that lead from a rustic lounge, opt for wood. It's about making the outdoor space an extension of the indoor area and it works much more effectively if the two areas are in tune. Chances are your crockery, tableware, vases, cushions and throws will all coordinate with the outdoor furniture if you operate this way.

Look on your outdoor space as a real part of the home and you'll reap the benefits of having lots of lovely extra space.

Q **I have put railings around my roof terrace but even with the furniture out there I don't feel it looks like a usable space. What am I missing?**

How did it go?

A *Is it that the space looks bare? Why not fix trellis along one or two sides and invest in a couple of potted trailing plants that will grow across the wood. This will give you an air of privacy by creating a natural wall. Is it that the space feels cold? Heaters that run on gas cylinders have come down in price over the last few years and now are within everyone's budget. Alternatively, and only if you are not going to have children around, what about an open air fire? You can buy stainless steel designs that house a central chamber in which you burn wood or coal. Finally, never underestimate the pleasing effect of a group of chunky church candles placed together in a group on the table.*

Q **I have a very long garden that I want to break into different levels. Any suggestions?**

A *You might want to think about terracing, which is the traditional way to create a series of different-level areas up the garden. This isn't a small job so be prepared for a lot of mess. It can be completed in a variety of ways, such as excavating areas completely, bringing in other materials to make up levels or by 'cutting and filling' where you use the waste from one area to build up the space in another. You'll need to approach a garden designer or builder to get a good idea of the costs involved, which will depend on how much digging and waste removal there will be.*

11

When white is right

Create chic interiors that will never go out of style. From pearly glazes to chalky finishes, the sheer variety of paints available means you can have a wide range of finishes when working with white.

It's a brave person that decorates a room with just white. But I would invite you to be bold because the finished look is truly impressive.

To open up small spaces and to create stunning larger rooms, white offers a stylish solution for every shape and size of space in the home. It can also be a good look when you are working to a tight budget. You can strip your old floorboards and wash them with white. You can buy junk furniture and give it a limed or antiqued white paint finish. And if your sofa and chairs are upholstered in a coloured or patterned fabric, you can throw swathes of plain cotton over them to bring them in line with the scheme.

You might think that your choice of colour will be limited. And if it was truly just a solitary colour you'd be right. But look at any paint chart and you'll see the range is vast. There are cool whites with a suggestion of blue, and warm whites that have an undertone of red or yellow. There are antique whites and contemporary whites, creamy whites and lime whites, and as already mentioned there are the different finishes to introduce too.

When you plan your white room, a good way to bring in lots of different textures is by your choice of fabrics. Consider a waffle cotton throw, white on white embroidered table linen and a muslin blind or curtains in the lounge. Introduce a canvas chair, a mohair blanket or a crewelwork bedspread in the bedroom.

Just pause for a moment and think about a variety of white things that you find in nature: tulips, eggs, shells, stone, milk and fur, to name but a few. Each of these has a different tinge and texture; each one presents a different facet of white, which just shows what tremendous variety this choice presents.

WHERE TO USE IT

All-white schemes have the biggest impact when you are working in a fairly large space. If you have tall windows, high ceilings and a generously proportioned room then you can use white to stunning effect. But the advantage of using it in small spaces like a box room or a tiny bathroom is that it will help to maximise available light.

Defining idea...

'White is not a mere absence of colour; it is a shining and affirmative thing, as fierce as red, as definite as black. God paints in many colours; but He never paints so gorgeously, I had almost said so gaudily, as when He paints in white.'
G. K. CHESTERTON

WHY TO USE IT

It's a scheme that will never go out of fashion. It suits both traditional Victorian interiors where you might want a warmer cosy feeling, and contemporary minimalist homes where you are hoping to achieve a cool mood.

HOW TO USE IT

When combining two or more whites in one room, keep the tone of all the elements the same. For example, if you used a white paint with a hint of pink on the walls, then avoid a greeny white fabric to cover your sofa. Make your choice of warm or cool tones after considering how much natural light there is in the room. South-facing rooms that benefit from plenty of warming natural light are the place to use the cool whites that suggest a hint of grey or blue. North-facing spaces that are darker and cooler for much of the day will benefit if you decorate them with whites that have a hint of pink or yellow.

- Warm whites: cream, buttermilk, limestone and ivory

- Cool whites: alabaster, eggshell, ice white and oyster shell

Be brave and go for an all-white look. You will grow to love it.

You can dress up a one-colour room with the right accessories. See IDEA 39, *The essential extras.*

Try another idea...

'**When the mists roll in and the leaves start to turn russet around the edges, white can still be warming and welcoming. Think of the inviting ivory glow from beeswax candles, a teetering pile of toasted marsh-mallows, a sumptuously thick cream-coloured chenille throw and a vase full of voluptuous white amaryllis scenting the air.'**
STEPHANIE HOPPEN, interior designer, *White on White*

Defining idea...

Q **I have used a browny matt white on the walls in the bedroom and then glossed the woodwork with a standard white. Now looking at the room the walls look slightly grubby. Why is this?**

A It is almost certainly the contrast of the two finishes. Your gloss paint is not only pure white but also shiny so it picks up the light, while your walls are not only off-white but also matt which appears to absorb the light. When painting walls in an off-white colour you ideally need to choose an off-white paint for the woodwork too. Lightly sand your woodwork and repaint it with satinwood or eggshell paint, or try painting over one wall with a pearlised glaze and see if this helps to marry the two together.

Q **I understand the idea of using different fabrics to introduce texture, but what else should I be looking for to dress the room?**

A When you are looking for pieces to include in your white room, search out pieces that are made from a mix of materials. I can't overemphasise the appeal of ceramic lampshades. They are a stunning way to dress up your lights. With furniture, search out Perspex tables, leather pouffs and white-painted wood pieces and choose sofas and chairs covered in linen or cotton. Finally, accessorise with frosted glass vases, a collection of white ceramics and groups of candles. I have seen a group of white tea lights placed in glass holders on a dining table with a length of fake pearls trailed around the bases – it made a great centrepiece for a table in a predominantly white dining room.

12

Decorative effects for a designer home

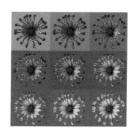

Walls, furniture, floors and sometimes fabrics can be transformed with a lick of paint.

TV makeover programmes may have given paint effects a bad name, but think again. For every change that you don't like, the screen designers that you watch come up with a good idea that you can use.

You may be weary of the format – horrid room, quick transformation, never want to live with it however will smile for the cameras – but every now and then you see a gem. These designers do have a trick or two up their sleeves.

Not convinced? OK, you are not obliged to watch any more TV. But please don't dismiss paint effects out of hand. They are easy, quick and above all else inexpensive. Also in my experience, if you want to make the best of your home – and why else would you be reading this – you'll explore any channel to achieve your desired look. The beauty of getting 'hands on' with paint is that you can adapt a piece of furniture or change the appearance of a wall to suit your style. After all,

Here's an idea for you...

Go to www.anniesloan.com Now you may have been tempted to skip this chapter because you think you will never want to pick up a paintbrush. I urge you to reconsider. As Annie says, 'With the simple addition of glaze medium to the paint mixture, a door opens onto a whole range of techniques, for it is what you use to make the pattern not the products themselves that create the finished effect. Using brushes, sponges, rags, combs etc. work to combine the base colour with the more transparent glaze colour on top. If you are not satisfied with the result then wipe it off and start again – before it dries!'

How easy could she make it – there's even the get-out clause at the end!

unless you have the funds to commission a one-off piece or pay an artisan, how are you going to get that junk table to fit in with your dining room décor or bring an original touch of the Bloomsbury Group to your living room? Basic rules that you may have heard before but need to be adhered to:

■ **Any surface** – wood, metal, fabric, plaster or fabric – needs preparation.

■ **Buy the right equipment for the job.**

■ **Read the instructions** that come with any product that you are going to use and stick to them – there's no cutting corners if you want the best look.

■ **Don't rush the job.**

■ **Practice on something/somewhere that doesn't matter** – the back of a drawer on furniture or a piece of paper for walls.

START SIMPLE

When I first picked a project, I looked for a piece of furniture that I could transform into an Art Deco drinks trolley. (In fact what I really wanted was a globe of the world that opens up to reveal the drinks – but there's no way that will fit in with my minimalist interiors so I compromised.) I assumed that adding a mirrored top and spraying it silver would work and completed the job in a day. *Hideous*. The point is to plan your work. Buy the piece. Sketch a picture of it – however crap you are at drawing – and then steal your children's crayons or buy a box of coloured pencils and make an attempt to create on paper a rough visualisation of the finished article. Then pin this up somewhere so that you will look at every day. If it's above your bed or on the back of the bathroom door then so be it. The front of the fridge works for me. Give it a couple of days and if you still like the look, then go ahead with your project. If it engenders gales of derision from everyone else in the house and you are not comfortable with it, then think again.

Where can you put your painted piece? IDEA 33, *A piece of the past*, will put it in a period setting and IDEA 2, *You've got the look*, shows how to set a particular style.

Try another idea...

> '**Remember that the most valuable antiques are dear old friends.**'
> H. JACKSON BROWN, Jr, American author

Defining idea...

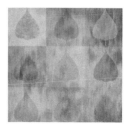

> '**One must act in painting as in life, directly.**'
> PABLO PICASSO

Defining idea...

KNOW YOUR LIMITS

It's unlikely that with one or two dribbles around the park you would expect to join Real Madrid. However if it was your first time with a football you might attempt a bit of Subuteo given the challenge. So try revamping a chest of drawers or a chair, but don't attempt to repaint every surface in your house in one go. It will take a while to get to the Bernabeu.

Pieces may need cleaning, stripping, sanding, filling, priming and smoothing before they are ready for the finish. And that final touch might be to distress, age, wax, stencil, lime, varnish, gild or decoupage depending on the effect that you want to achieve.

Research the type of look you want: an aged, antiqued or really glossy finish and paint effects offer a stylish solution for decorating your home.

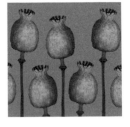

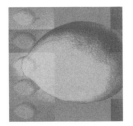

Q **I have picked up an old chest of drawers that I am thinking of painting but I paid a lot of money for it, so should I paint it?**

A *The answer to that is 'don't paint serious antiques'. There is nothing worse than a Lloyd Loom chair that has been bastardised with paint. If you paid good money, chances are that it needs repairing or renovating rather than a complete facelift. When you buy from junk shops check for the following: wonky legs, worm holes or broken hinges and locks that don't work. If you can restore it without changing the overall appearance so much the better. In general, items that are cheap – MDF, some wicker, plastic and pine – might be worth giving a coat of paint.*

Q **I have been thinking of gilding a chest of drawers but am aware that working with metal leaf can be tricky. Any tips?**

A *The preparation is the key as any imperfections on the surface will show. Make sure that you have sanded the area that you are gilding to a smooth finish. Use wood filler on any dents or deep scratches and ensure that the surface is free from dust before you start work. If you are painting the piece first, apply two or three coats and sand with wet and dry paper in between each coat. If this is your first time, you might want to avoid metal leaf and use gilt cream instead which you can simply rub on with your finger.*

How did
it go?

13

Introduce Scandinavian style

Create the perfect setting for your Norwegian Blue. With the combination of countries that make up Scandinavia you can expect an eclectic mix of different styles, but the paired down, clean and fresh, typically termed Swedish look is my choice.

Why? Because it is versatile, simple to achieve and easy to live with — all welcome attributes in anyone's book.

Think rustic wood. Think simple printed cottons. Think fresh blues or muted reds and you are looking along the right lines. More importantly, this style calls for a mix of old and new so it doesn't need to cost a fortune to achieve the look.

FIRST CHOICE FABRICS

One of the most important elements of Swedish style is the use of material. You can happily introduce check, stripe, print and patchwork all in the same room, as long as the colours match of course. A quilt with plaids in navy, red and white is the perfect piece to use as a starting point for your room. Pick out a coral colour from one square and paint a wooden chair to match. Find a blue that you like amidst the checks and use a plain fabric in the same shade to make curtains or a blind. There is

Here's an idea for you...

Take a trip to the southeast of Sweden to Sundborn where you'll find the home of Carl and Karin Larsson. You'll see paintings by Carl, textiles woven by Karin and furniture that she has designed. The interior is a source of inspiration for interior designers across the world. Check out the tourist board website for travel and accommodation information.

a place for delicate sprigged florals, traditional gingham and even classic ticking in this room.

SOFAS AND SEATS

The finely turned legs and elegantly carved backs that are synonymous with this style owe their genesis to a prince. Back in the eighteenth century when Gustav returned to Sweden (to become King Gustav III) after living it up in the Court of Louis XVI, he brought back the classical form of furniture that he had seen in France.

History lesson aside, that's not to say that you have to invest in stacks of expensive antique furniture. You'll find many furniture companies make designs along Gustavian lines that you can paint yourself. But you can also look out in junk shops or reclamation yards for any sofas or chairs that have simple, clean lines, straight backs and legs that taper to the foot. Give them a coat of clean white paint, reupholster in a pink or blue check or add throw and cushions, and you've got a piece that cheats the look. If your sofa is the wrong colour, you can get away with using a tie-on loose cover in cream or white for this style.

ESSENTIAL ELEMENTS

Wood panelling figures large. Add MDF pieces to dado level or try tongue and groove up to picture rail height. If you are designing a small room, use high-level flat skirting so that you don't shrink the space too much. All mouldings should be simple in style; avoid anything that is curly or looks too ornate.

Stripped or painted wooden boards are the flooring of choice. But you can afford to put down simple runners or rugs to break up a large expanse of floor space.

If you love rooms with a very clear style, this look offers an easy to achieve finish.

'Create your own visual style...let it be unique for yourself and yet identifiable for others.'
ORSON WELLES

Defining idea...

For more advice on choosing and using rugs, see IDEA 43, The best dressed floors are wearing...

Try another idea...

'In a progressive country change is constant; change is inevitable.'
BENJAMIN DISRAELI

Defining idea...

How did it go?

Q **I have the right fabrics and furniture but the room just looks like it's decorated in blue and white – it doesn't say 'Swedish'.**

A *You obviously have all the main elements in place but you need to add some finishing touches. A shelf running around the room at picture rail height will give you the perfect place to display Carl Larsson prints or blue and white china - both key accessories in a Swedish-style room. Simple wood mouldings added to the top of plain cupboards, the front of cabinets, along the edge of shelves and even to table legs all mimic the Gustavian style.*

Think about where you have positioned the furniture. One key part of this look is the symmetry of the room, so place a chair either side of a cabinet with the backs flat against the wall. Or put a footstool either side of a window to frame that part of the room.

Q **I'm still not sure it looks Swedish...**

A *Carl Larsson was saying 'Chuck out your chintz' years before it became a catchphrase for a Swedish superstore. Embrace the idea that you are going to strip things down to the basics - a clean white wooden floor, a sofa with an upholstered back and neat clean lines to the silhouette. Colours are simple, and so are the rest of the elements in the room. Remember that the finishing touches show an eye for detail rather than a place for clutter. When you put a collection of china or a group of pictures in place, take a step back and just make sure that they work in the room.*

14

Tread softly, because you tread on my dreams

Or where and why to use carpet

These words of Yeats always makes me think of curling my toes into a super-thick pile carpet. It may not have been what he had in mind when he was wishing for the cloths of heaven but it works for me.

The soft solution for flooring underfoot is a fail-safe choice for bedrooms, my recommendation for lounges, and can be used anywhere else in the house as along as you buy the right type for the amount of wear and tear it will receive.

One day, I'm going to have a huge carpeted bathroom. I just love the idea of climbing out of the bath and stepping onto a soft floor for a change. I've walked across enough vinyl to appreciate the difference but I know I'll need to find a design that will withstand the wetness.

Here's an idea for you...

If you have the budget, get the best of both worlds by putting down a wood floor and then adding a large unfitted carpet on top. If you choose a light oak or beech floor and opt for a dark carpet on top, it means you can instantly change the look of the room by keeping the carpet down in cold winter months and then rolling it up and storing it through the summer months.

Familiarise yourself with the jargon of carpets before you buy. The construction, pile, fibre content and texture are all points to consider. Clearly your biggest influence will probably be the colour but these other things need to be factored in. You want a carpet that will last so check a couple of things to give you an idea of how hardwearing it will be. Look at the back of woven carpets and make sure that the tufts are packed closely together. Kneel down or press the pile with the heel of your hand and make sure that it springs back quickly. Good quality woven carpets are sure to last. If you choose a tufted design, go for the most expensive you can afford.

If you are carpeting the whole house and need to cut costs, go for less expensive carpets in the bedroom and spend more money on areas that get constant use such as the hall, lounge and stairs.

THE PROS OF CARPETS

While wood floors have become overwhelmingly fashionable, it's important to remember the benefits that a carpet offers:

- **Keep the noise down:** It dampens down sound between floors and from foot traffic – a real bonus in flats. According to The Carpet Foundation, bare smooth flooring is likely to produce seven to twelve times more noise than a carpeted surface.

- **Cosy up:** It provides insulation for your home – any kind of energy saving is a priority in today's environment.

- **Whoops a daisy:** It offers a cushion for falls, and a non-slip surface to prevent accidents.

The choice of colour of your carpet will have an impact on the mood of the room. See IDEA 3, *Work that colour*, for more on colour scheming. You can add interest to the room by including one or two rugs. If you want to dress up your carpet, see IDEA 43, *The best dressed floors are wearing...*

Try another idea...

'*What if everything is an illusion and nothing exists? In that case, I definitely overpaid for my carpet.*'
WOODY ALLEN

Defining idea...

A DESIGN TOOL

With so many colour choices and such a wide range of textures, carpet is a valuable decorating tool when putting together your scheme. Because of the large amount of space that it covers, plain carpets in light colours will help to make a room seem much bigger. Using the same carpet through two or three small rooms will also create the illusion of a bigger home. Patterned designs have their place if you have kids or pets, helping to disguise wear and tear. If you have opted for plain walls and furnishings in a room, they also function as a tool for bringing in a mix of colours to the area.

Budget for good quality underlay: it prolongs the life of a carpet. It levels out any imperfections in the sub-floor, and is an effective way of preventing heat loss – on average 15 per cent of heat loss from a home is through the floor. The thickest underlay is not necessarily the best, however. Look for one that has been made by a carpet manufacturer from the yarn that is left over from the carpet-making process for a high quality option.

You want to walk over your floors in comfort for years to come so take the time to carefully consider the carpets.

Q **I have looked at a wide range of carpets and if I buy a wool mix it is going to cost a fortune to carpet my room. Why shouldn't I buy a cheap one and be done with it?**

How did it go?

A *There is no point in buying cheap carpet. It doesn't wear well and you'll have to replace it so quickly that the cost of buying another new one and having that fitted means you might as well have spent more in the first place. There is also a suggestion that synthetic fibres pose a health risk as a source of volatile organic compounds (VOCs), common indoor air pollutants that can cause allergies. Blow your budget on a high quality stain-resistant wool mix and you'll be able to live with it for years.*

Q **That's all well and good, but once I have spent a fortune how do I care for it?**

A *There's a dull job that has to done on a regular basis – vacuuming. If dirt is left to embed itself into the pile it will age the flooring. You can brush floors and sweep floors but really giving it a good going over with a suction pump (that's a vacuum to you and me) is the best solution. Bear in mind that heavy furniture will leave indents in the carpet. The image of little cups under legs may seem old fashioned, but they do do their job.*

15

Keep it tidy

Decluttering is the new black. Whether you want to make extra space or simply clear up your home, get set for a brutal experience.

There is a way of tackling tidying that lacks commitment. It involves tucking papers in drawers, putting magazines back in the rack and working on the assumption that 'I might use it one day'.

Stop right now, thank you very much, in the words of the immortal Spice Girls. If you are going to declutter you need to approach it with dedication and verve and most importantly, with a lack of sentimentality.

Pick a room – any room – and sit in the middle. What you are about to do is remove roughly one-quarter of the contents in that space. That's your target. (And that's just for starters. Once you have performed your initial declutter, if you are really serious about it I want you to go back a week later and repeat the process.)
In the kitchen: you are chucking out unused spices, old tins, battered bakeware, chipped crockery, fraying table linen, knackered saucepans and unused gadgets

Here's an idea for you...

You may want to look at another book in this series, *Detox your finances*, which has a very useful chapter on selling items on the web. 'Car-boots in cyberspace' explains the complexities of the e-bay auction and how you could make money out of your junk.

(bread makers and juicers being chief culprits). In the lounge: you are getting rid of books on the bookshelf (that's where the sentimental bit comes in for me; I hate getting rid of books), China ornaments that were dodgy holiday mementoes or suspect gifts, dried flower arrangements, worn out cushions and old CDs. In the bedroom: you are looking to give many, many items of clothing to the charity shop. If you keep your bed linen in there, how many sets do you realistically need? If you've mislaid one of a matching pair of pillowcases chuck the odd one out – if you take it downstairs to the kitchen to cut up and use as cleaning cloths you are only adding to the clutter down there, so chuck it.

In the bathroom: it's time to dispose of old make-up, old medicines, half-used body lotions and potions and towels that were stained by your last hair-dyeing experiment. It's all very well thinking 'I'll use that at the beach', but when was the last time you remembered to take a spare towel with you?

It's a process that is loosely based on the William Morris principle 'Have nothing in your houses that you do not know to be useful, or believe to be beautiful.' And it makes absolute sense. Most of our clutter is just a home for dust and dirt.
So here's how to approach the job. Start in the corner furthest away from the door. If there's a rug on the floor or a cushion that needs to go, take it out of the room and put it in a pile outside the door. If there's a cupboard in the corner, open the door and, starting from the top, take out everything that's on the shelf. For each item ask yourself when was the last time that you looked at it, read it, used it or

even thought about it. If you can't remember any of the above then take it out of the room and add it to the pile. If the cupboard is not sectioned off, bring in some new storage systems: box files for papers, garments bags for clothes, etc.

The key to decluttering is having good storage. IDEA 49, *An organised mind*, **explains the essentials.**

Try another idea...

I should mention at this point that it might be worth having a bottle chilling in the fridge, because you will need an incentive after and hour of two of doing this. Also, in the same way that people jog to pacey music or work out to funk, make sure that you are listening to something inspirational. I mix up a bit of Barry White, some Stone Roses, very early Michael Jackson and a bit of Bruce Springsteen. It all gets me moving one way or another.

Don't give up when you get bored: the aim is to clear the excess baggage in one sitting. You have to look on it as a job that needs completing before you are allowed that glass of wine, not reach for the bottle when you are halfway through. Take everything that you've removed and recycle it in the appropriate way.

Approach decluttering with the determination of a pitbull and you'll reap the rewards in terms of tidiness, cleanliness and lots of lovely extra space.

'Be ruthless with your wardrobe. We wear 20% of our clothing 80% of the time; so make sure the clothes you move are the things you wear. Give away any garments that you haven't worn in the past year.' 'Life Laundry' presenter DAWNA WALTER, *Your Home*

Defining idea...

'When we got into office, the thing that surprised me most was to find that things were just as bad as we'd been saying they were.' JOHN F. KENNEDY

Defining idea...

How did it go?

Q **I have tried to empty my house of excess bits and pieces, but I'm left with piles of papers that I can't be parted from my work area in the lounge and clothes all over the floor in the bedroom.**

A *You have obviously embraced the principles but please check that you can't get rid of these bits. Go for your second declutter and see if you do really need everything that's left. Failing that, you may need to consider bringing in extra storage. Built-in wardrobes in the bedroom are a brilliant solution for making the most of the space and keeping it free of a clutter. A table with drawers underneath could be just what you need to provide extra storage space in your lounge.*

Q **I understand that, but how am I going to make storage in my study area fit in with the rest of the lounge?**

A *Do you have a dedicated office-style filing cabinet? You don't need to have a piece of furniture that doesn't fit in. Designs are available in wood instead of metal if you are worried about the utilitarian look of metal designs, or you can paint them with a coloured aerosol paint to fit in with your colour scheme.*

16

The sun also rises

Brightening with yellow. When the sunshine pours through a window into your room you can forget your troubles for a while.

There is a reason why Judy followed the yellow brick boad and it's because such a sunshine colour offers a wealth of positive associations.

If colours were people then yellow would be the happy gang. Orange, its close neighbour in the colour spectrum, would be the go-lucky crew. If you need something positive in your life, these are the colours that you should look to use for positive energy and a more invigorated and energy-filled approach to life.

Of course, there's always that occasion when you could happily punch the person who has a permanent smile on their face. That jaunty builder who heckles you with 'Cheer up love, it might never happen' (at which point I always have to resist the temptation to tell them I've just been divorced and the dog has died, but I digress). The point is that sometimes you can have too much of a good thing, and for that reason there are occasions when it's good to avoid using too much yellow or too bright a sunshine shade – in your bedroom for example. It's a full-on colour and

Here's an idea for you...

If you live in a basement flat or have a north-facing room your priority is to make the most of any available light. Choosing yellow for these rooms will boost whatever sunshine reaches the dark recesses of the room. Another point to consider is that often basement or ground floor flats or rooms will have low ceilings. You can create the illusion of height by painting the ceiling a lighter shade than the walls. Try blending colour up the wall. If you have a dado or picture rail then start with a darker yellow beneath the mouldings, choose a lighter shade above, and go for white with a hint of yellow or a creamy white at the top. (If you have the opposite problem try reversing this technique. Move from dark at the top to lightest at the bottom and the ceiling will visually seem lower.) Use mirrors on walls facing the window to reflect light into the space.

one that could set you back hours if you are overstimulated when your body and brain have only just regained consciousness from hours of sleep. It may leave you feeling slightly grumpy and disorientated because you don't exactly know why you are not up to speed. If you do choose yellow for the bedroom, pick a warm primrose colour, which is cheerful enough to kick start your day without being too loud. Clotted cream woodwork will also tone down the effect.

My advice is to choose bright yellow for rooms where you want to be motivated. A sunshine yellow kitchen or dining room will have you cooking up a storm and entertaining guests with inspirational tales. More importantly, it is a warming colour and can be used to counteract the negative effects of being in a north-facing home or a basement flat.

DESIGNS IN COLOUR

Some colours lend themselves to certain
patterns, and for yellow it's stripes. A delicate
way of introducing yellow to a room is by
choosing wallpaper with the slimmest primrose pinstripe. The Laura Ashley
wallpaper collection has a wonderful colour called Cowslip. It's a creamy yellow far
removed from the brash and bright primary colours in this sunny family. You can
also use an orange stripe, although it will have the effect of bringing a retro mood
to the room, while the yellow choice will create the mood of a summery country
cottage. (If you like the retro look you must see the Ted Baker Wallcoverings
collection. Better known for his shirts and swinging Elvis Santa at Christmas, the
coverings are set to become classics.)

For brightening up dull rooms and bringing a spring to your step, consider a yellow
colour scheme.

**For an alternative scheme to
lighten spaces, see IDEA 11,
When white is right.**

*Try
another
idea...*

**'Busy old fool, unruly Sun,
Why dost thou thus,
Through windows and
through curtains call on us?
Must to thy motions lovers'
seasons run?'**
JOHN DONNE

*Defining
idea...*

73

Q   **I've used yellow and white throughout the living room but it seems when I walk into the space the mood is bland, not bright.**

A   *It maybe that you were scared to use a bold shade and have gone for a wishy washy colour. One way to liven up the look is to bring a completely contrasting colour into the space. Try raspberry. You could use some blooming floral prints arranged in a group on the wall or a modern 'work of art'. One of the easiest ways to introduce these spots of colour is with flowers so pick up a bouquet of blooming peonies or some lush tulips and position them on a shelf or mantelpiece against the yellow walls. You'll instantly appreciate the difference.*

Q   **My room is already very bright as it gets the sun morning noon and night. Can I still use yellow?**

A   *You are so lucky. If you have a space that has that much natural light then you can rely on white with a hint or two of yellow to decorate the space. If you think of yellow as an accent, something to bring out the flavour of the room in the same way that a touch of chilli brings out the flavour of certain foods, then you'll realise that you don't want to drench the room with it (it would be too hot) but a pinch here or there is a great way to conjure up a visual feast.*

17

Bathe in style

Washing, crimping, bathing or refreshing – a well-designed bathroom is a versatile space.

Lie in your bath and take a good look around you. The starting point for planning a new bathroom can often be a list of the faults of the existing one.

I inherited a particularly hideous over-the-bath shower with elaborate shower rail system to allow the curtain to be pulled all the way around the bath. It was totally unnecessary, and the poles suspended in a mish-mash from walls and the ceiling made it look like an elaborate industrial mess. By simply taking away the curtain and associated poles and putting in a neat screen I made the room seem instantly bigger, and it's now definitely more pleasurable to lie in the bath and gaze at the ceiling, or my navel.

If you are going to revamp a bathroom, you need to decide whether you want to keep the existing layout and replace fixtures where they are, or move things in, out and around to get better use of what is, more often than not, a spatially challenged room.

Don't panic if you have inherited a coloured suite with co-ordinating tiles. The chances are it's so old that you may want to replace it, but even if it stays you can detract from the hideousness of the tub and walls in various ways. Tile paint is much maligned. Yes, it is a laborious job to recover tiles and no, it won't look as good as replacing all the tiles, but if you prepare the surfaces religiously and follow the instructions as if they were commandments, the finished effect is pretty good. Use in conjunction with tile grout pens and you can refresh the room. Alternatively, you can buy panels with a tile design already imprinted on the surface and these can be fitted over the top of existing tiles.

Clear out anything that isn't white or neutral. Towels, laundry baskets and cupboards should all be replaced with neutral colours (in the case of cabinets, a glass fronted design, maybe frosted, is particularly pleasing on the eye). And consider putting in a new floor. In general the dimensions of the room are so small that it won't cost a fortune to put down new vinyl.

SUITE PIECES

I am a bidet fan and not ashamed to admit it. Let me give you some uses (other than the purpose it was designed for) to explain why, if you have the space, I would recommend that you fit the fourth piece into your suite of bath, basin and WC.

- There's always somewhere to leave the hand-laundry soaking.
- It is the perfect place for washing feet pre-pedicure.
- If you can't use the loo to be sick you have another receptacle.

With both bidets and toilets always opt for wall-hung designs, for one simple reason: cleaning around pedestals is a pain, and they are a place where dirt tends to gather. The joy of being able to mop across a floor unhindered by the usual obstructions has to be experienced to be really understood. (If you are now worried that I am slightly obsessive about fluff on the floor, I'd like to point out that I have a dog whose hair tends to get everywhere.)

It's a frequently overlooked issue that cast-iron baths weigh a ton (give or take a few pounds). If you are looking to recreate the look of a period

If you are going to replace the flooring take a look at **IDEA 28, *A tough decision.***

Try another idea...

'Colour is incredibly important to me, but in the bathroom that means the opposite of what you may think – everything's got to be white. When you're trying out every colour of every item in a make-up range, it's essential to have a neutral background. So the idea of coloured lights and fancy tiles is all well and good, but it's just not for me. And no, I never had an avocado suite.'
BARBARA DALY, *The Independent Magazine*

Defining idea...

bathroom, check that your floor will take the weight. Also remember that with a freestanding bath the amount of water that splashes over the edge will increase considerably (more sides for the bath water to slop over) so you do need flooring that will withstand regular soakings. While the idea of picking up an old fashioned piece from reclamation yards may have a romantic appeal, don't bother. Brand new is easily affordable and reproduction designs are so good that I would buy new every time.

SINKING IN

If you live with a partner or have kids, fit in a double sink wherever possible. There is great pleasure in having your own sink. I once stayed in a glorious hotel in Edinburgh for New Year where the bathroom had 'his and hers' sinks. My contact lens solution, make-up, body lotion, electric toothbrush and cotton wool pads all had a space, and didn't get shoved aside when 'him indoors' wanted to shave. Now translate that into your own home. Kids' stuff on one sink and adults' on the other for example – it's a cleansing experience.

Q   I have roughly planned the layout of the bathroom but there isn't enough space along one wall to fit in a sink and a bidet. Also, with a towel rail on one wall and the tiles above the bath on the other, the window on the third and door on the fourth, what can I do about storage?

How did it go?

A   *Take another look at your plan and see if it's possible to put a corner basin at either end of the window wall. It may need to be slightly smaller than the sink you have chosen, but it has the benefits that if it is fitted into the top of a cabinet you will gain extra storage as well as free up wall space for your bidet.*

Q   I've opted for an all-white room but in winter it feels desperately cold. The walls are completely tiled so I can't introduce a warmer colour with paint. Any ideas?

A   *Instant changes can be wrought. Invest in some towels in warm colours – ruby red would be perfect. Try bringing in some natural wood and wicker in the form of a cabinet, towel rail or linen basket. Put a rug on the floor; use something with a rubber backing so that it won't slide around. And invest in toiletries or accessories in pink, orange and red: soaps, oils or candles, whatever you fancy.*

18

People in glass houses...

Forget that image of a tacky white plastic extension on the back of a house in the suburbs: conservatories can be gorgeous.

This is particularly true if you are lucky enough to have a south- or southwest-facing garden that will allow the maximum amount of sun into the room.

If you are in this position I really recommend that you start saving or go and get a loan straightaway to pay for the job. You will have the luxury of an extra room in your home all year round and one that, if planned and decorated with care, will become the most popular room for reading, drinking and chilling out (or getting a bit of privacy if you're lucky).

THE PLANNING GAME

Ignore anyone who says that you need to decide on the use of your conservatory before it is built. This is nonsense. After all you don't just cook in the kitchen, you also eat, entertain, argue and do laundry. In the lounge you may have supper on your lap, watch the television, read or fool around (you can do that last one in the kitchen too). The point of putting in an extra room is to give your home some extra

Here's an idea for you... **Find furniture that you like, rather than feel the need for dedicated conservatory pieces. You might see a better selection of tables and chairs in the garden section of your local DIY superstore than on a specialist conservatory furniture website, for example. Fading is obviously an issue in a room that is exposed to the sun so don't spend a fortune on fine fabrics for cushion covers. Lightweight pieces are clearly a priority so that you can move them around the room to maximise hours sitting in the sun. I have seen the prettiest wirework tables and chairs used in a conservatory – reclamation yards might be a good place to check out – and you can dress these up or down according to the season with cushions and throws plundered from other rooms in the house.**

interior space – what you choose to do in there will certainly change through the seasons and very probably through the years. You can decorate it, accessorise it, and furnish it in such a way that it can fulfil multiple roles.

First consider the following:

Budget. Spend the max to get the best. Bear in mind that blinds can eat up a large chunk of money if you are fitting them across the whole extension.

Which way will it face? North – will need attention paid to heating and lighting for the winter months. Ask your installer about specialist types of glass that will offer extra insulation. South – good quality blinds or shutters are essential for the summer. Good ventilation is vital too, so plenty of roof vents and some opening windows. Consider tinted glass for the roof. East – it will catch the morning sun so use materials that retain heat, like thermal glass. If you are thinking about an extension to the kitchen this will give you the perfect breakfast room. West – make sure ventilation is good to prevent condensation from hot evenings and cold nights.

Shape. How much of the garden and which area are you willing to give up? If you have a small side passageway that leads to the garden but serves no other function why not start to extend there and use that wasted space? If you are seriously spending, consider a two-storey affair.

Material. Make it blend in with the rest of your house. Here are the options. PVC – durable and virtually maintenance free. This is often installed in white but you can find wood-look options. This is the C-list celebrity of the conservatory world. Aluminium – strong, so can support large predominantly glass structures but may be prone to condensation – the B-list candidate. Timber – what it loses in terms of ease of maintenance it gains in versatility and style. A-list (Oscars, all the best parties, Gstaad in the winter, St Tropez in the summer).

Just like outdoor spaces, you want to get maximum use out of your conservatory. IDEA 10, *The great outdoors*, will give you some useful hints for co-ordinating it with the rest of the house.

Try another idea...

'The butler opened a door for me and stood aside. It opened into a vestibule that was about as warm as a slow oven. He came in after me, shut the outer door, opened an inner door, and we went through that. Then it was really hot. The air was thick, wet, steamy and larded with the cloying smell of tropical orchids in bloom. The glass walls and roof were heavily misted and big drops of moisture splashed down on the plants.'
RAYMOND CHANDLER, *The Big Sleep*

Defining idea...

'If slaughterhouses had glass walls, everyone would be a vegetarian.'
PAUL McCARTNEY

Defining idea...

Heating. Underfloor heating is the best. You don't see it but you know it's there and in winter you'll be glad you have it. Choose this option if you are going to lay ceramic tiles or stone flooring. Radiators are another option. You may be able to simply add them on to your existing central heating system if your boiler has the capacity for the extra work. Or invest in one or two oil-filled radiators, which are quite an efficient way of heating if you can't extend your existing system.

A conservatory can mean a substantial financial investment and you want to use it all year round, so get the basics right from the start.

Q   **We have just started using our newly built conservatory but the condensation in the room seems excessive even after I have opened windows and left a heater on. What can I do about it?**

How did it go?

A   *For the first few months after the building has been completed it is drying out so levels of condensation will be particularly high. These will reduce after 6–12 months; during that time you should keep the windows open as much as possible. Keep the heating on low for a few nights, especially through the winter months (warm air holds more moisture than cold air). You could invest in or hire a dehumidifier for a week or two and accelerate the drying out process.*

Q   **Can I just build on to my house or do I need permission to extend the property?**

A   *This all depends on where you live, and size also matters. If you live in a conservation area you will almost certainly need planning permission. You may also need Building Regulation approval on certain designs, for example, if it is a kitchen conservatory. Your builder or conservatory designer should be able to advise you, so get this query out of the way before you start planning your extension.*

19
An illuminating experience

Get the lighting right and it can be the making of a room; skimp on this essential design detail and you may end up in gloom.

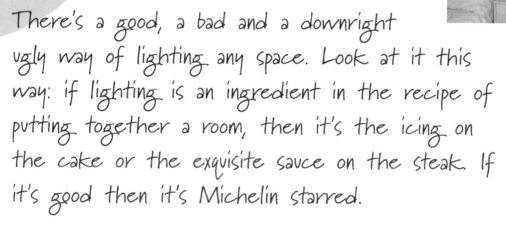

There's a good, a bad and a downright ugly way of lighting any space. Look at it this way: if lighting is an ingredient in the recipe of putting together a room, then it's the icing on the cake or the exquisite sauce on the steak. If it's good then it's Michelin starred.

If it's bad you may have perfected the main part of the dish but the overall meal will be just average. And if it's downright ugly then you have ruined the meal. You waste all the effort of putting together a lovely interior if you fail to pay attention to how the space is lit. Lighting ties quite neatly in to how the area will be used. Every room in your home serves a variety of purposes, so allow for an assortment of lighting options to fulfil each and every need. Lighting also has a role in drawing attention to specific features in a room, and the reverse of that is that it can be used as a means of disguise by leaving certain areas in darkness.

Here's an idea for you...

Do you have a collection of objects on a shelf or an amazing print on the wall that could be highlighted with a specific source of light? Firstly move a lamp near to the piece and send the beam so that it casts light straight on to the group. That may be too strong. Point the beam down and see what effect that creates, and then position the light source so that it shines up towards the group. Each position of the light will create different shadows so play around until you have the most pleasing combination of light and shade.

SORTING THE STYLES

You can reduce lighting to three basic types, and to create a successful scheme you need to layer all three: ambient, task and accent lighting. Ambient light is designed to offer an all-over well-lit room. This is the starting point to any scheme and the most basic type of lighting. Task lighting, as the name suggests, works to illuminate specific tasks. These might be working at your computer, applying your make-up or cooking. Its purpose is to provide enough light for the activity concerned – enough to prevent eyestrain. Accent lighting is the type that can often be neglected but brings out the best in a room. It will highlight the best features such as works of art, pieces of furniture or a particular area – a dining table in a kitchen/diner is a classic example.

ROOM BY ROOM

The first space that you come to in a home is the hall. Do something different on the stairs. Position a recessed spot light or low-level wall washer beside every second or third step, making sure you have an on/off switch at the bottom and top. Moving into the lounge, why not avoid an overhead light altogether and have an electrician put two or three lamps on a circuit that is operated by a single switch? If you have shelving in alcoves either side of a chimneybreast, then use down-lighters to highlight the items that are displayed. Through to the kitchen, make sure that you include lights that run underneath wall-mounted cabinets as well as your overhead strip or spots. Have the different lights on separate circuits so you can use as much or as little light as you need. This will also mean you can transform a practical and functional working area into somewhere appropriately lit for an intimate dinner party. Jump up the stairs to the bedroom, and you must have lights at either side of the bed. Move to the bathroom and make sure that you can see to cleanse your face. An illuminated mirror is a must.

When dressing up your home, lighting is an essential tool in creating the right look and style for every room.

There is an art to lighting and displaying objects. See IDEA 30, *The art of living*, for some ideas on grouping pieces and positioning pictures.

Try another idea...

'Sometimes our light goes out but is blown into flame by another human being. Each of us owes deepest thanks to those who have rekindled this light.'
ALBERT SCHWEITZER

Defining idea...

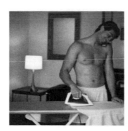

'It is not economical to go to bed early to save the candles if the result is twins.'
Chinese proverb

Defining idea...

How did
it go?

Q **I know that I need to mix up different kinds of light in a room but where do I start?**

A *Let's take the lounge. If the only source of light is a central pendant fitting then you need to do some light work. The first step is to fit a dimmer switch. It's a basic step but it does mean you can lower the lights to create a subtle glow. Next, while there are no fixed rules, if you can introduce downlighters, uplighters, wall washers and lamps you are well on the way to improving the look of your room. (You'll be familiar with all of the above except possibly wall washers. These are lights that cast an even glow across and down a wall.)*

Q **I have mirrored tiles on one wall in the bathroom and I am getting a real glare rather than a pleasing glow when I switch on the overhead light. Even putting in a low wattage bulb hasn't really cured the problem. Any suggestions?**

A *I presume that you operate the light with a pull switch at the moment. If you have the space, try putting in a wall cabinet with integral light on the wall opposite to the tiles and use this rather than the overhead light when you are in the room. Another option would be to get an electrician to come in and move the control to the outside of the room. Then you can use a dimmer switch (safety regulations mean this type of fitting should be outside the room).*

20

Bold reds make for instant impact

Or...la vie en rose. From the hottest scarlet to the subtlest pink, this palette can create instant impact or a subtle glow.

The woman with the red Chanel lipstick makes a striking statement in a crowd; the girl with the English rose complexion takes more time to spot and longer to appreciate; but both have their inherent appeal. So it is with rooms where you choose to use red.

Are you decorating your den? Work with claret and create a cosy space – somewhere you'll retreat to when you feel cold or even lonely.

The mere act of enveloping yourself in a room of ruby shades suffuses the body with warmth. I'm not becoming an advocate for any therapy that takes you back to the womb, but you'll get that safe and warm feeling in a lounge decorated in Tudor red. When I plan a room with red, I embrace these historical associations. I think of it as somewhere that will look well worn, like a dusty old library or one of those

Here's an idea for you...

When was the last time you ate Neapolitan ice-cream? If you really want to work with pink, then think of vanilla-, biscuit- and rose-coloured ice-cream melting together into scrumptious fluffy shades. This is your modern look for pink. The very nature of these pastel colours will dictate a feminine feel to the room but you can counteract that with clever use of fabrics. If your walls are painted in pink, choose a biscotti brown suede sofa in the lounge or a cappuccino-coloured fabric for your bed head. Then add a creamy sheepskin rug to go in front of the fireplace or a heavy cream eiderdown to throw over the bed. Allow just enough pink pieces to peak through, be they crisp cotton bed linen or taffeta and silk-style cushions to pull the look together.

wonderful country house hotel bars where you have a Kir before going into dinner.

I would advise you to avoid department stores when looking to furnish such a room. Try auction rooms or second-hand shops where you can pick up old and worn leather pieces and wooden tables, chests and bookcases that might show the odd knock or scratch. A battered Chesterfield is the perfect piece to place amidst deep red panelling, an oak side table the ideal spot to stand your crystal decanter filled with the finest port. Look for cushions and throws in chocolate brown and consider an old tapestry or hand-embroidered pieces to add to the comfortable air. A pair of rich velvet curtains will complete the look – hang them from a chunky wooden pole.

SUBTLE COLOURS

The delicate shades of pink, synonymous with a perfect English rose, are as much in contrast with the above colour scheme as chalk and cheese. While deep reds suggest passion and power, pink has lighter associations: the Pink Panther, tickled pink, in the pink – a sign of good health. There was a trend a few years ago for shabby chic: the look that relies on pretty chintzes, antiqued white furniture, rag rugs, a sort of tatty Laura Ashley catalogue from years gone by. This is the perfect style for using pink. A feminine look – no, not girlie, more a room that is comfortable with its age and knows it still looks good. If I say to you it's Katherine Hepburn, while the bolder reds would be Sophia Loren, does that give you a clearer idea?

This is about a subtle use of the colour, more simple touches than whole swathes of a certain shade, because I firmly believe no one (with the exception of girls under eight) would want to – or probably should be allowed to – decorate an entire room in pink.

So, in the kitchen it could be a pink gingham blind at the window above a cream butler's sink, or a collection of rose-patterned china in a farmhouse glazed top or open rack dresser. In the hallway it should be a scalloped edge lampshade atop a simple white candlestick base on the consul table, or a flower in the print of a heavy chintz curtain that covers the front door when it's closed. In the bathroom it could be the soaps, lotions and potions that adorn an open shelf, maybe the ribbon edging on fluffy white towels.

Working with red gives you the opportunity of creating real impact with a colour scheme – don't blush at the thought but go for it.

'When in doubt wear red.'
BILL BLASS, American fashion designer

Defining idea...

If you want another way to use pinks and purples, see **IDEA 26**, *Welcome to my boudoir.*

Try another idea...

'The true colour of life is the colour of the body, the colour of the covered red, the implicit and not explicit red of the living heart and the pulses. It is the modest colour of the unpublished blood.'
ALICE MEYNELL, poet

Defining idea...

How did
it go?

Q   **I've painted all the walls in red but the room now seems to have shrunk to about half its original size. What can I do to reverse the effect?**

A   *If the room was small to begin with it may be that you will need to rethink your colour choice because such a strong shade will visually shrink the room. Get two people to hold up a white sheet against the wall at the far end of the room (or use a staple gun to temporarily hold it in place). You'll see by lightening the colour there that it immediately changes the perspective of the space. So the first thing to do is paint the wall that is opposite the door (the first wall you face as you walk into the room) in a lighter colour. Choose any neutral – a soft grey, off-white or beige are all options. Alternatively, do you have a dado or picture rail? Experiment with changing the colour in one of these areas, again to a neutral colour.*

Q   **So I know I want to use some red, but any tips for introducing just a touch?**

A   *There's no reason why you can't introduce any style or colour in small doses. If an all-red room seems a bit too much, then use it on a small scale. Red can be added to alcoves or the occasional architectural detail: skirting boards, picture rails and cornices spring to mind. Just take a step outside. What would your house look like with a bright red front door? Now there's a bright idea.*

21

Something's cooking

Take the fitted approach to streamline your kitchen. The beauty of investing in a fitted kitchen is that it can be tailor-made to suit all the quirky corners or awkward shapes that exist in most homes.

It's also a way of maximising space and can provide some brilliant storage solutions, designed to make your life that much easier.

With the luxury of starting from scratch you can make sure that the light is right, that the power points are in the correct places for all your gadgets, and that your day-to-day use of the space is a joy. After inheriting a kitchen that had clearly been built by the previous owner's DIY-mad husband, I rejoiced when my kitchen had to be ripped apart. Oh the joy of a new beginning!

I have to say at this point that when you move into a new home, budget often precludes you from investing in a whole new kitchen however much you might hate the previous owner's colour scheme or layout. By using paints, replacements doors and perhaps a new floor, it's possible to give the room a facelift that might make it more bearable. You'll just have to live with the layout, but buying a freestanding kitchen trolley is one way of getting an accessible work surface if that is what you lack. However, we are dealing here with the extravagance of a whole

Here's an idea for you...

The list of requirements is complete, but have you overlooked some aspects of the room?

Could you lose a pan cupboard and make it the space for storing equipment by having a rack suspended from the ceiling for hanging up saucepans? Have you had to reduce the number of cabinets in a run because there is a radiator on the wall? You could take it off and have plinth heaters instead. Have you had to devote a chunk of work surface to house a large microwave? Choose a built-in combi-oven that includes a microwave facility.

Defining idea...

'Some of our most exquisite murders have been domestic, performed with tenderness in simple, homey places like the kitchen table.'
ALFRED HITCHCOCK

new design so be clear about your budget before you start. Costs can easily run away with you and a cheaper option is always available for most things.

THE TRIANGLE PRINCIPLE

This is an age-old device that kitchen planners have been promoting for years when they start to lay out the room.

It goes like something like this: the cooking area, preparation area and storage should each be at the point of a triangle so that you can move efficiently between the three work areas. I choose to ignore it because everybody cooks in a different way. While the sink may be one of your three important areas if you don't own a dishwasher, if you do it means your priorities will be different. And with microwaves replacing ovens for a lot of people who reheat ready-made meals, that lovely high-tec fan/gas/electric combi-cooker may only be used at the weekends. You want a layout that suits you for more than two days a week. I like space in my kitchen so have fitted everything along one wall to leave the rest of the room free of cabinets. It's a simple 'line' design with the cooker, sink and fridge positioned along the same side of the kitchen in a run. That way I can move easily and 'crablike' along the work surface and between the three – take potatoes out of the fridge, wash them in the sink and put them on the hob to boil. I predict I will save myself (over several years) hours and hours of running backwards and forwards across the kitchen. Well, quite frankly, if I needed that much exercise I wouldn't be cooking with real cream and butter.

MAKING PLANS

If the number of people hanging around the Ikea kitchen department on a Saturday morning is any indication, you'd think putting together a kitchen required a degree in design. It doesn't, but the sheer volume of options for cupboard doors, work surfaces, appliances, etc., can be intimidating. It does help when you are planning a kitchen, probably more than any other room in the house, if you can make a decision. If you are the kind of person who takes half an hour to choose which toppings you want on your pizza, give yourself a year to put your room together.

Considering that cooking, eating and even watching TV all take place in the kitchen, it's worth spending time to put together your perfect room.

Does your kitchen double up as the dining area? Turn to IDEA 29, *Eating in is the new eating out*, for some hints and tips on combining the two functions.

Try another idea…

'The doorway led into a short hallway, lined with closets, and then into the butler's pantry, lined with glass-front cabinets containing sparkling battalions of crystal, and stainless steel sinks. The cabinets, with their beadings, muntins, mullions, cornices – he couldn't remember all the terms – had cost thousands… thousands… And now they were in the kitchen. More cabinets, cornices, stainless steel, tiles, spotlights, the Sub-Zero, the Vulcan – all of it the best Judy's endless research could find, all of it endlessly expensive, hemorrhaging and hemorrhaging…'
TOM WOLFE, *The Bonfire of the Vanities*

Defining idea…

Q   It all sounds too much – there are so many things to consider. Where do I start?

A   Let me make it more approachable. Break it down into the following areas: cooking, storage, preparation, washing up and eating. Compile a list of all your requirements in these areas and you're well on your way to designing your kitchen.

Q   I have designed the kitchen with some interior-lit cabinets, but how do I know if I have adequate lighting in the room?

A   One way to guarantee that you have enough light in the room is to include a track system on the ceiling, fitted with swivel spot lights. This means you can always point a beam in the right direction.

22

Blind ambition

Simple lines and a structured design make for the perfect window dressing. A lovely window treatment doesn't have to rely on swathes of fabric.

The beauty of blinds for me is that they sit neatly in their designated space. You know where you are with them; there's no tweaking of tiebacks or messing with a pole and rings.

Once a blind has been installed it's a straightforward up and down, or down and up routine, and if you think they are too plain, then think again. A patterned fabric made into a blind can have just as much impact as a dressy curtain.

I have an intense dislike of wooden Venetian blinds. I think it's because they can be used at virtually any window so people use them far too much. I always feel that no thought has gone into the window treatment when I see it dressed up like this – it's as if someone has taken the easy option and hasn't even considered that a softer blind might be better suited to the room.

So please think about how you dress your windows. They may be at the very edge of any room but they can take up a large proportion of the wall space and need the same consideration that you give to your paint colour or choice of wallpaper. Which

Here's an idea for you...

Vertical blinds make brilliant room dividers. If you have an open-plan living/dining room and want to break up the space to create added privacy or more clearly define the two uses of the areas, they can fit neatly across an alcove or can be suspended from a fitting in the ceiling. This is a more contemporary approach then putting in folding doors. Choose a colour that is close to the paint or paper on the walls.

Consider your choice of material when buying blinds for the kitchen and bathroom. Look to use wipeable PVC blinds in the bathroom where they may get splashed on a regular basis. In the kitchen, and for safety reasons, make sure the blind is made in fire-retardant fabric.

brings me neatly to a point that you will want to consider. If your walls are painted in a single colour, you can use your choice of blind to introduce an interesting contrast to the space. If you have chosen to hang a patterned paper, then a plain blind may be just what you need.

CHOOSE A STYLE

I'm not sure it is even worth discussing festoon blinds. Does anybody still choose this frou-frou style? Perhaps I'll just say that if you were unfortunate enough to inherit one when you moved into your home, then you should take it down this instant. Pin up a sheet instead. Roller blinds bring simplicity to a window – just a flat piece of fabric that neatly rolls away. Dress up a plain roller with a contrasting panel at the bottom, or if you are a fan of stencilling they provide a perfect canvas for your work. If you are thinking about a treatment for your bedroom and need to preserve your privacy, choose a bottom-up design. With a box fitted to the window sill (preferably), or outside the bottom of the frame (this can look bulky), you raise them up rather than drop them down. This means the bottom half the window can remain covered while the top is clear to allow light into the room. You also have the option of combining an opaque panel with another material, perfect for a lounge that is overlooked.

One of the greatest new innovations for rollers is the huge variety of pulls from which you can now choose; wooden blocks, jute balls, leather laces and ceramic beads can all be added to the bottom of your blind if you feel the need to dress it up a bit.

Have a look at IDEA 36, *Softly, softly,* for ideas on using different types of fabrics.

Try another idea...

All of my windows have Roman blinds. How boringly unimaginative of me. It's because I love their clean lines: the way that the pleats sit neatly when they are open and the way that the fabric lies flat when they are closed. I like to be able to choose any fabric I want so rather than buying from a catalogue I always buy my own material and then have them made up by a professional curtain maker. It's an approach I would recommend because it doesn't cost a fortune. You can buy an inexpensive fabric to compensate for the making-up costs and once it is up no one will know that's where you cut costs.

Reefed blinds make a more quirky statement but can end up being a pain to operate and keep looking neat. These are pulled up and down by cords, which run through eyelets at the top of the blind and loop down and around the fabric. This means you can pull them up very tight, but you often have to fiddle with the fabric to allow it to roll up neatly. It's the sort of blind to use at a window where it may stay half down for any number of days.

If you pick the right design of blind your windows will always look good.

'Relying on the government to protect your privacy is like asking a peeping tom to install your window blinds.'
JOHN PERRY BARLOW, retired rancher and cyber rights activist

Defining idea...

101

How did it go?

Q   My kitchen window is in a recess. How do I know what size I need?

A   *You can measure up inside or outside of your recess. If the window you are dressing is flat, then measure across the frame; if it is recessed, then you need to measure between the walls at either side or in which case you can make the blind as big as you want.*

Q   How do I know which style to choose for my kitchen?

A   *Well, as we have discussed, I would ignore anything very flouncy. Roman blinds are a great option in a kitchen because there is very little material to trap dirt and dust and they can be made in almost any fabric. This means you can match them to the colour of your cabinets, your floor or anything else you choose. The design means that they are simple to operate so you can get them out of the way of wall-mounted units or the cooking area.*

23

To sleep, perchance to dream

Design your bedroom with comfort in mind. While buying a house may be the biggest financial investment we make, buying the right bed is one of the most important.

Really. Sleep deprivation caused by a crying baby, pressure of work or a snoring partner may not be easy to resolve, but if it is a direct result of an uncomfortable bed, then the solution is in your own hands.

But more of beds later. Let's consider just how you want your bedroom to look and how to achieve that before we get into the specifics of furniture. Start with the style, which will dictate colour choices, fabric types and furniture design, and bear in mind that there are endless variations on these themes.

RUSTIC LIVING

Bring the comfort of the country into your bedroom. Yellows and greens or rosy pinks can form the basis for the scheme. Keep a light touch when decorating. Opt

Here's an idea for you...

Some notes about buying beds...

- **Buy the largest bed you can fit into your bedroom. That way you and your partner will have your own space to sleep in.**
- **If you and your partner have different requirements, then consider investing in two different mattresses that will zip together.**
- **A hard mattress is not necessarily a good mattress. What you are looking for is the right amount of support. Lie on your choice for a good few minutes before you buy.**
- **Turn your new mattress every time you change your bed linen.**
- **Forget fashion – is the height of the bed you are buying right for you?**

for wallpaper with a delicate print, and if you can't face papering every wall, then just use it in alcoves or on the wall facing the door. Choose carpet for the floor and reflect that cosy mood with wool blankets on the bed or a patchwork quilt that matches your colour scheme. Indulge yourself with a curvy wrought iron bedstead and plump for painted or pine wooden furniture for storage. Lamps with pleated fabric shades would be apposite for the bedside table, as would a blanket box positioned at the end of the bed.

CONTEMPORARY ROOMS

The art of Feng Shui and the influence of the Orient have had tremendous impact on interiors, and nowhere more so than in the bedroom. Work with a colour scheme including white, shades of grey, cream and brown. The mood is minimalist so hide or disguise clutter in the room. Opt for a laminate or real wood floor that you can dress up with rugs for extra comfort. Select natural linens to deck out the bed, calico or cotton pillowslips, for example, and put wooden Venetian blinds or shutters at the window. A low-level wooden bed would suit this style, and fitted wardrobes would contribute to the clean lines of the space.

CLASSIC LIVING

Consider a muted yellow or duck egg blue as the starting point for your scheme. It may be appropriate to pick a patterned carpet so you will need to choose your bed linen to co-ordinate accordingly. Curtains are a must. If you want to add a dressy pelmet at the window then echo this look with a canopied bed and be lavish in your use of fabric. Feel free to introduce a gilded mirror or arrange classic prints across one wall. It suits the mood to display a collection of perfume bottles or perhaps have an antique set of brushes and hand held mirror on display. A slipper chair, fabric-covered ottoman or chaise longue will add the finishing touch.

Next consider how you will layout the room. Can you create a focal point with the bed or will you rely on architectural features such as a fireplace to draw the eye? Maybe you have invested in a magnificent old armoire that you are going to use for storing clothes and linen, or have a dressing table that will sit in the bay of a window.

Where are you going to put the mirror? Don't leave it out but don't just stick it on the wall. Consider a freestanding design or a large framed mirror left on the floor to lean against the wall.

If you want some inspiration in your choice of accessories, see IDEA 39, *The essential extras*, for ideas to dress up your bedroom.

Try another idea...

'The bed is a bundle of paradoxes: we go to it with reluctance, yet we quit it with regret; we make up our minds every night to leave it early, but we make up our bodies every morning to keep it late.'
OGDEN NASH

Defining idea...

105

Where are the lamps? A reading light mounted at either side of the bed or lamps positioned on bedside tables will add symmetry to the space.

Given that we spend up to a third of our lives in the bedroom, it is worth getting a style that works morning and night, summer and winter to fulfil every requirement.

How did it go?

Q **We have bought a new low-level bed but now our old bedside cabinets are too high for us to use. The budget's virtually all spent, so what can we do?**

A *Can you scrape together enough to buy two cheap occasional tables? Simply cut down the legs to the height that you require. Alternatively find two tablemats (leather or glass would be ideal). Take them along to your local wood merchants and get two blocks of wood, as near to the height of your bed as possible, cut to their dimensions. Paint the wood to match your colour scheme and place the mats on top.*

Q **What do I do if I can't budget for a new bed?**

A *This is tricky because there is nothing worse for your body than a second-hand bed. I am going to suggest a compromise – a new mattress on top of an old frame, although no one who is worth their salt in bed design or sales would agree. You could look for a frame in a junk shop – hospital and old school dormitory beds might suit the guest room because they are sturdy but will not be used that often. Remember that ideally a bed has only a 10-year life, so while you may need to save money, don't expect someone else to sleep on a bed that would give you nightmares.*

24

The green room

Create a cool, calm and collected mood. In colour therapy green is the colour of healing and growth. It's calming and restful and brings balance to the soul.

Now that I know this, I understand why I feel so much better when I have a piece of lime tucked into the top of my beer bottle, and why when I don't I can get very, very angry.

It's also a lucky colour, so invest in some green underwear for when you go to buy your next lottery ticket or go to watch your team. But how does this affect where we use it in the home?

If you consider the choices in the green group, many of the colours are inspired by nature. There's the previously mentioned lime, plus evergreen, moss, grass, avocado, apple, clover and fern. The list goes on and on.

Choose paler shades of green when you want to make a room seem larger. Introduce it into spaces that face west or southwest and need cooling down to counteract the heat from the sun. Introduce it on the wall where patio doors lead into the garden and you'll find it has the pleasing effect of picking up on the colour

If there is a particular area in the home which you would like to make more relaxing, paint one or two walls with a light green wash. Bring in some houseplants, not spider plants, but a bamboo or glossy ficus tree. Get two or three green throw cushions and chuck them on chairs or the sofa. The soothing effects of this quick makeover should be felt straight away.

of the foliage outside, thereby unifying the two spaces. It is that reflection of nature that contributes so much to the restful effects that the colour can achieve. It is also why it works so well with other natural materials like bare wood, stone, wicker and cotton.

Use your imagination for a minute. Picture a well-scrubbed pine wooden kitchen table. The backdrop is a combination of cupboards dragged in a light green wash of paint and the floor is a pale limestone flag. Copper-coloured pans hang from a ceiling rack and a light gingham check dresses the window. Doesn't that sound appealing?

Defining idea...

'Green Eggs and Ham *was the story of my life. I wouldn't eat a thing when I was a kid, but Dr Suess inspired me to try cauliflower.'*
JIM CARREY

Now go into a lounge where the walls are papered with a slim green stripe. The two sofas that face each other across a low-level maple coffee table are covered with loose cream cotton covers and the floor has a sisal-look carpet. A mirror is framed in faded grey driftwood and the wooden shutters at the window are painted white. Doesn't that sound relaxing? These are the reasons to use green.

Give green it's due: decorate at least one room using this scheme for a well-balanced and relaxing home.

If you are thinking about painting wood furniture to match your green scheme, see IDEA 12, *Decorative effects for a designer home*, on the rules of using paint effects.

Try another idea...

'Green is the colour associated with the fourth chakra, located in the heart area, and so is connected to matters of the heart. On the physical level, this includes the functioning of the organs close to the heart region, such as the lungs, the chest and the whole circulatory system. It can be helpful for someone suffering from asthma or bronchitis. Green also helps to balance the flow of blood, and it is interesting that doctors and nurses often wear green gowns in the operating theatre.'
CATHERINE CUMMING, *The Colour Healing Home*

Defining idea...

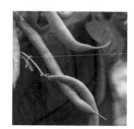

Q   Right, I understand that I need to calm down, but where are the best places for green?

A   *Green is a good choice for the bedroom, where you want to be calm. If you have a hyperactive child, try decorating their room in green and you might be surprised at how positively it can affect their moods. It's also ideal for kitchens where you can sometimes get stressed out over the cooking. Because it's a cool colour it can also counteract the effects of all that heat and steam.*

Q   I have decorated a couple of rooms in green but while they are relaxing to spend time in, I also sometimes long for a little more stimulation.

A   *It sounds like while you might never want to leave your sanctuaries of calm, you're finding the overall effect a little too laid back. If you have found these ideas just a bit too mellow, you may want to introduce a contrasting accent colour to add a bit of zing to the room. Opposite green on the colour wheel you'll find red, orange and purple in varying degrees. If you think about the impact that a vase full of purple and green irises can have, then you're working along the right lines. Introduce a vase of purple flowers into a green lounge. Alternatively group together a collection of purple candles on a table in front of a green painted wall. Leave a bowl of red apples in the middle of the green kitchen's table and pile up a platter with red cherries – it certainly adds a vibrant touch.*

25

A professional opinion

There are some occasions in life when you have to call in the experts. Whether you need an architect, builder or estate agent, they all need managing.

Looking to improve your home, create extra space or merely flog it? It is certainly wise to rely on trained professionals to help you in your quest, but how do you know you are going to get the best service and not run into one of the following scary scenarios?

'I paid the 10% deposit in cash and never saw them again', or 'the architect says the building time is running two weeks over', or 'its been on the market now for three months and we haven't had an offer anywhere near the asking price'.

HOW DO YOU AVOID THIS?

Don't be scared of them! The technical terminology may be confusing but pin them down until you understand exactly what is going to take place, when, how and for how long.

Here's an idea for you...

Draw up a shortlist of possible architects and then request a portfolio from each one. You will get a much clearer idea if you can compare and contrast work at the same time. Use this opportunity to get a list of their qualifications and any references from previous commissions. That way you have all the information you need before you make your final choice.

It's all in the planning and channels of communication. Get these right from the start and the experience should be bearable – let's be realistic: it's never ever going to be a joy letting someone else get involved with your space, but the least you can do is try to set up the situation so that it doesn't end in tears. In practical terms that means a time-line for builders and architects and a clear understanding of how the estate agent is going to market your home.

BRICKIN' IT

If builders were obliged to carry ID cards and register with a professional body, it might solve some of the problems associated with the trade. Here's my advice. Keep a logbook of the job. It needs to be dated – add times if it seems appropriate – and you need to keep a comprehensive list of who does what on the job. This is in addition to any contract that you sign. You can use this log to compare against the progress of the agreed timetable. (In addition to the costs and outline of the work involved, look for a start and completion date, a start and finish time each day, any safety and security provisions and an assurance about the disposal of any waste materials.) This advice comes from harsh experience. One team not completing a job properly and another team then also failing to finish it left me with a leaking roof. If you can pinpoint exactly who is responsible you will stand a much better

Defining idea...

'When one has finished building one's house, one suddenly realises that in the process one has learned something that one really needed to know in the worst way – before one began.'
FRIEDRICH NIETZSCHE

chance of getting things finished satisfactorily. You also stand a much better chance of success if you name the individuals concerned rather than referring to them generically.

You'll need a builder if you choose to put in a conservatory, see IDEA 18, *People in glass houses...*, for some more information.

Try another idea...

BUILDING IT

In the best scenario an architect can manage the job, dealing with the subcontractors who are working on your home. First and foremost, when you want to use an architect look at as much of the finished work of the firm as you can. Their style will influence your style. You might meet a 'glass and steel' man who you get along with famously but will the finished design work on the extension to your country cottage? It's all about building up a relationship so that you have a mutual understanding and respect. Architects can be relied on to cope with any legal requirements that you may have to fulfil, knowing who to speak to in order to get planning permission for example.

Be strict with them about your budget. Costs can easily creep up when you are choosing materials, for example. A granite worktop will elevate the costs of a kitchen extension dramatically and there are thousands of alternatives.

Defining idea...

'Got home, late and exhausted, to find Gary the Builder still there and house completely taken over with burnt toast under the grill, washing up and copies of the Angler's Mail and Coarse Fisherman all over the shop. 'What do you think?' said Gary, proudly nodding at his handiwork. 'They're great! They're great!' I gushed, feeling mouth going into funny tight shape. 'There's just one little thing. Do you think you could make it so the supports are all in line with each other?'

HELEN FIELDING, *Bridget Jones: The Edge of Reason*

SELLING IT

Do estate agents always have your best interests at heart? It would be in a perfect world (no wars, no plagues, no famine) where they did. No of course they don't. The commission cheque looms large over any negotiation. There's your starting point. Haggle over how much you are going to pay them. If it's a large chain which offers advertising in its own brochures or local press, a web presence and window display you're going to pay a little extra, but if you don't actually like being passed from one agent to another you might be better off going with a one-man band – at least you always know with whom you are dealing. The highest value isn't necessarily the best. An agent can inflate a price to get your signature on the contract (and get your hopes up of trading up) but then the price will have to be dropped to get a sale and you may be left short for your next purchase.

Q **I have seen several architects and narrowed my choice down to two companies having seen their portfolios. I need to provide them with a brief for the job so that I can get a more definite idea of costs. How do I approach this?**

How did it go?

A *You should by now have a clear idea of the work required so grab some magazines and compile a selection of tear sheets that show the style, materials, colours and rough size of the job. With this include a list of your expectations, how the space is going to be used and how soon you want the job started/finished. Copy this to both companies and you should by their respective responses be in a position to make your final selection.*

Q **Contract aside, how do I know that they are going to do the job well for me?**

A *A good builder should be able to supply you with references from satisfied customers. You may even want to go and look at some work before you employ them. Check the finish on any job. If they are running late they may not give the finishing touches the same care and attention as the rest of the job.*

26

Welcome to my boudoir

Think glamorous, think gorgeous, think about a sexy and sensuous space. If you hate design rules and like to mix things up then boudoir style is for you.

It conjures up for me a mix of rich fabrics, curvaceous furniture and a room filled with all sorts of unusual accessories. It is laid-back and bohemian and it embraces a wide variety of materials in its style.

In boudoir style, you won't find many straight lines or a structured layout to a room. What you may see is a pile of cushions spilling from an old chaise longue onto the floor where they double up as footstool or seating when required. A bed will be dressed with a silk bedspread and a mixture of pillows in different shapes and sizes. Detailing on furniture in the room is curly and ornate, and positioning of these pieces takes a fairly random approach: they don't have to be flat against the wall but can sit at an angle in the middle of the floor. If you have a chest of drawers or desk that you think might fit in terms of shape, then you can replace plain wooden knobs with glass ones to fit with the look. In the same mode swap wooden shelving for glass and change plain supports to a filigree design. If boudoir style is

Here's an idea for you...

Try using pearlised paints on one wall in the room. This finish comes into its own if you position a lamp so that the light catches the reflective surface.

applied to the bedroom you might find an antique wrought iron washstand alongside a battered armoire. If it's in the lounge there could be a velvet-covered slipper chair sitting beneath a wall-mounted candle sconce.

With the flamboyant nature of this style of room you can afford to go a little over the top when dressing up the space. If you like the idea of a fabulously fluffy sheepskin rug, then position it beside the bed or in front of your hearth. Faux fur throws and cushions can find their place across the bed or draped over sofas and chairs. Include baubles, trinkets, embroidered cushions and old lace. Go to antique arcades and rummage to find interesting pieces, or raid the old family home for an heirloom or two.

Look out for:
- Mother of pearl accessories
- Antique gold frames
- Coloured glass and pearl-glazed lustre ceramics
- Anything with a beaded trim

COLOURS AND FINISHES

Work with a palette of purples and pinks. Look for richly coloured beaded silk cushions or trim plain ones with lengths of organza ribbon. There's no doubt this is about indulging your feminine side so make the most of really pretty pastel shades. You might also want to consider a course in gilding if you are serious about working with this look. A touch of gold here and there in the room creates just the right sense of decadence for this style, and you can add it with gold leaf, wax or paint to a variety of surfaces once you know the tricks of the trade. Take an old wrought iron garden chair, for example, and add patches of gold to the frame. Have a little round cushion made up to fit the seat so that it feels like it belongs inside the house. You can also use a length of silky fabric to wrap around the back and legs of a plain wooden chair transforming it into a lavish and stylish piece.

There is a place for reflective surfaces in this room. Can you track down one of those wonderful Venetian-style mirrored console tables where the drawers are etched or painted with a floral design? If not get a suitably decorative mirror. You are trying to find something with a rippled edge or a design that has an elaborate motif at the top and bottom of the frame.

If you want to live with a relaxed atmosphere and missed out on the tidy gene, boudoir chic could be just your thing.

Boudoir chic is perfect for the living room, but if you want some more suggestions for this room, see IDEA 38, *Lounging around.* *Try another idea...*

'As she sallied forth from her boudoir, you would never have guessed how quickly she could strip for action.'
WILLIAM MANCHESTER, American historian

Defining idea...

'Poetry is a mirror which makes beautiful that which is distorted.'
PERCY BYSSHE SHELLEY

Defining idea...

Q   My whole house is fairly bohemian and I've pulled together this look in the lounge by combining lots of different bits and pieces from the rest of my house. The one thing I am lacking is some boudoir lighting. What should I be looking for?

A   *What you want is something really flamboyant. Your choice of light fittings is crucial with this look. A chandelier is essential for the sumptuous mood of the room. Try and find a design that has been dressed with murano glass drops or add your own crystal drops. You can drape a length of fake pearl beads between two fixtures for a decorative touch. Candle style fittings for the bulbs are something to look out for, or get decorative bulbs not plain designs.*

Q   I've got the basics but it needs a few frills.

A   *Remember that it's the quirky details that contribute to the overall appeal of this look. It's OK to drape a fringed shawl over the end of the sofa or leave a silky nightdress hanging from a pretty padded hanger suspended from the front of your armoire. Be relaxed and laid back and you'll get the look that you want to achieve.*

27

Young at heart

When you design a child's bedroom you want a space that can adapt as they grow.

And boy do they grow. From the toddler who has no say in how you decorate their space to the independent child who wants it all her own way, you need to create a flexible scheme.

Not having kids of my own I don't have first-hand experience, but with nine nephews and nieces I can lay claim to some knowledge of the subject. If you need to give the room a single priority it has to be storage. A couple of drawers under the bed and a set of crates for toys makes a good starting point but however much storage you start with, multiply it three- or fourfold and you'll be getting close to the real demands that will be made on the space over the years from baby to toddler to youth. You can stop worrying there because after that it's pretty much up to them what goes on. A teenager's space is a sacred retreat – enter at your peril.

A WORK IN PROGRESS

Start with some basics in the room that will stay in place for several years. It has to be said that a good quality carpet is worth the investment as it will be crawled over, played on and might even have to survive the odd drenching from a drink thrown

Here's an
idea for
you...

Fabric drawstring bags provide practical storage for everything from clothes to toys. They make a versatile option and bought in different colours and designs are one way of adding colour and fun to the room. The quickest and easiest way to add lots of extra storage space is to put up a peg rail around the room from which you hang any number of bags. Make sure that when you put it up, you drill good deep holes and use rawl plugs for extra strength. You have to figure that at some point children will pull on bags and put the rail under considerable pressure.

mid-tantrum. Any cheap flooring just won't withstand that much wear and tear.

Next think about your choice of bed. You can buy cots that convert into a child size bed. They may be pricey but make a good long-term investment. If you choose to buy a cot and then replace it when the child has grown out of it, you are looking for a bed that will last for ten years. That's about the maximum life span for any bed anyway, but if you spend wisely at the beginning you won't have to worry about it again for sometime. A bed that has another mattress which slides out from underneath, with legs that pop up to make another bed, is a sensible choice given that you are bound to have to provide more sleeping space at some point for pyjama parties.

Don't bother to wallpaper the whole room. If your child requests a paper with a favourite football team, cartoon character or doll, then buy a roll and use it on just one or two walls so that when they get bored with a design you aren't stuck with repapering the whole room. Paint the remaining walls in a neutral colour that will work with other changes in the place. Hardwearing finishes are essential so why not add tongue and groove around the bottom half of the room? (Also that way you would only have to wallpaper the top half anyway.) If you paint it in a hardwearing oil-based paint it will also be stain resistant and easy to wipe clean. Alternatively opt for a wipe-clean vinyl wallpaper which cleans with the sweep of a wet cloth or sponge.

Be realistic about how many times you want to refurbish the room through the years. Baby-sized furniture is very cute, and all well and good if money is no object, but I suggest you invest in 'grown-up' pieces from the start. If you want to change the handles on a wardrobe or the knobs on a set of drawers with suitably cutsie designs, it's a considerably cheaper way of making the furniture match the room. Look for pieces with lasting style and ones that could, should you wish, be repainted to update them – pine wardrobes and MDF shelving spring to mind. Bookcases, chests of drawers and blanket boxes are all valuable sources of storage in a child's room. They will be there for several years.

For more ideas on choosing carpet, see IDEA 14, Tread softly, because you tread on my dreams.

Try another idea…

If you are thinking that it all sounds a bit boring for children, then the list of goodies that are comparatively cheap to buy and easy to change runs something like this:

- Lampshades
- Bedlinen
- Blinds
- Bean bags / floor cushions
- Rugs
- Fabric wash bags
- Door / drawer knobs

'What might be taken for a precocious genius is the genius of childhood'
PABLO PICASSO

Defining idea…

You can happily let your children choose these according to their current passions, which at certain ages can change as quickly as their shoe size.

Choose practical and durable furniture and furnishings and your child's room will last through the ages.

'All the time a person is a child he is both a child and learning to be a parent. After he becomes a parent he becomes predominantly a parent reliving childhood.'
Dr BENJAMIN SPOCK

Defining idea…

How did it go?

Q **I have finished the room but my daughter is a light sleeper and even if I draw the curtains they let in too much light during her afternoon sleep. They co-ordinate with the rest of the fabrics in the room so I don't want to replace them. What other option do I have?**

A *You have a couple of choices depending on how you have hung the curtains and what type of window you have. If there's a recess, then have a roller blind made in black-out fabric and fit this to the frame. Alternatively, pick out a dark colour from the pattern and buy another pair of curtains to match this and hang them from a supplementary pole.*

Q **I indulged my son's choice for Super Heroes wallpaper but he's now into football and wants a change. Any ideas?**

A *Buy some of those little football stickers and position them randomly among the heroes. Then explain that even Super Heroes need play time and tell him he can change the room when he's ready to redecorate it himself.*

28

A tough decision

Choose stone floors for their looks and durability. In my fantasy world where money is no object, marble floors are available to everyone and limestone and slate find a place in the appropriate space.

I'm talking about lovely great big slabs of the stuff. Not neatly cut, squared off tiles (they are the subject of another chapter in the book), but substantial, large and lengthy pieces that take a mountain of a man, or more probably several, to move.

Have you seen the recent version of *The Thomas Crown Affair*? (One of the only remakes, incidentally, that comes anywhere close to being as good as the original.) Piers Brosnan and Rene Russo have a passionate session on the stone staircase in Thomas Crown's immaculate apartment. Now that's not the everyday sort of punishment that you subject your stairs to, but it is an example of how floors can be put through some pretty vigorous workouts. The great news is that you can rely on most hard floors to offer the ultimate in durability and this contributes much to their appeal. (That, and you don't get carpet burns.) If you are subjecting a hall to

Here's an idea for you... **There is a world of difference between the supplier and fitter of a floor. Someone sourcing stone may well have a life-long love affair with the product and an intimate knowledge of its quirks and qualities. They'll know how to coax out the best features and disguise any failings. A fitter is there to lay the floor whether it's marble, slate or limestone. If one company is providing the complete service, all the better. If you are sourcing the stone from an importer and getting someone else to fit it, then make sure your supplier gives you some back-up. You'll need the proper sealant and a specification sheet with details on how to treat the stone which can be passed on to your fitters.**

constant traffic or a kitchen/diner to regular entertaining, then a hard floor can take the punishment when a softer option might show signs of wear and tear.

There is something about stone that says timeless luxury. Is it because we know that these materials have formed over millions of years and so deserve to be treated with the respect and deference that their age commands? (There is a small quarry in central France, for example, where limestone is extracted from beds which were laid down in the early Jurassic period some 140 million years ago.) Or is just that we are familiar with seeing them used in grand houses and historic buildings which make them an object of desire?

WALK ON BY

Marble is to floors what diamonds are to jewellery: an expensive choice but one that rewards you with its sheer beauty and dramatic impact on the eye. In sheet form it is always going to break the bank (sort of like a four-carat emerald-cut stone), but there is the less pricey alternative of tiles, although these are more likely to be a backing material with a veneer of marble laid on top. Marble is one of those materials that makes a real statement. It needs to be used in big spaces and grand locations. That's why you find it used in luxury hotel foyers.

Granite is in the luxury goods department too. The choice of colours, from pink-hued and speckled white to blue-grey and black, means it can fit in with most colour schemes. Can I say it's rock solid? Well it really is incredibly hard and will be in place for longer than you or I will be able to enjoy it. Just be careful if you choose a polished finish as this will make it slippery. (Again, it's available in tile form, which would make a really good choice for a hallway or vestibule.)

If you are wondering about terracotta or mosaics, IDEA 48, *A night on the tiles*, addresses these materials.

Try another idea...

'Joseph Ettedgui, innovative retailer and fashion entrepreneur, believes that lighting and flooring are the two most important elements in the home and if these work, "everything else will look wonderful". Whenever he is creating a home, he always spends as much money as possible on good quality flooring, whether stone, wooden parquet or the softest carpet. "The floor is one of the very first things you feel when you enter a place", he says. "Your feet actually feel quite a lot."'
SIR TERENCE CONRAN, *Easy Living*

Defining idea...

'Nothing is built on stone; all is built on sand, but we must build as if the sand were stone.'
JORGE LUIS BORGES

Defining idea...

127

Slate has a much more rustic appeal, and if you want an immaculately smooth finish to your floors look elsewhere. It can be slightly rough with worn edges, but its waterproof qualities makes it a good choice in the bathroom, for example.

For those of you who are looking for a lighter option, you should be asking about sandstone and limestone. In creamy whites, buttery yellows and pale grey, these would be suited to areas where you need a floor in keeping with a light colour scheme. (Some of these are named after the area in which they are quarried just to confuse you: Cotswold stone, for example is a limestone.) Now if these floors are laid properly, sealed and maintained they will look great. However, because they are porous they will easily stain so make sure that you get them treated. For that same reason you must also be careful about the type of cleaning solution that you use. A black mark in the middle of a large expanse of light stone will ruin the luxury look, and you can't just scrub it off with bleach.

Here's an idea for you...

Q You say that stone must be sealed properly, but with what?

A *It can be any product that penetrates the upper surface of the stone and and protects it from dirt and scratches. Your supplier or installer should be able to supply a special stone floor sealer. Once that is done you can always apply something extra – on slate, for example, a water-based, self-polishing wax can be applied over a sealed floor for extra protection.*

Q Right, but how do I then clean the slate?

A *The best way to keep it clean is with regular vacuuming to get rid of any grit and a weekly mop over with a damp (not sodden) mop. If you need to apply detergent make it a really weak solution and rinse it well.*

29

Eating in is the new eating out

Relax at home with a dedicated dining space. Why the rush to run out with your credit card and pay for a meal that might or might not be worth the monthly interest?

A friend of mine recently went to the new and highly lauded restaurant set up by a young chef to train teenagers with no skills (social or work that is) for a career in the catering industry.

Now the food wasn't great but they drank enough wine to dull the edges of their disappointment and made it from start to finish without sending back a single dish. When the bill arrived my friend's husband grabbed it as the couple they were out with had just recently decided to get married. 'Look on it as our engagement present', he said. The words were hanging in the air, like one of those cartoon bubbles, as he opened up the bill. It was astronomical, I mean more than enough to feed a small nation. His response was to burst out laughing. Sometimes when you feel you've been taken for a sucker that's the best response. When I heard about it all I could think was 'imagine how many takeaways I can eat at home with that amount'. (Also, how much good wine I could buy, because we all know that the mark-up on a restaurant wine list is enormous.)

Here's an idea for you...

If investing in a matching set of chairs is beyond your budget, go for an alternative. Buy four or six wooden chairs from junk shops. They can be all sorts of shapes and sizes but *must have* removable fabric-covered seats. Take out the seat and remove the fabric. Lay it on a piece of paper and cut round to give yourself a paper pattern. Then simply position this on a new fabric, cut out your squares and centre the seat cover on top. Fold over one fabric edge and staple to the underneath of the seat. Then do the same with the opposite edge. Make sure that you keep the fabric taught. Repeat with the other two sides and put back in the chair. Repeat for all your seats – and now you have a matching set.

Now I'm not saying that there aren't many, many occasions when we want to go out and eat. I crave the social atmosphere and general *bonhomie* that being in a restaurant generates as much as the next person. But what I am suggesting is that if you set up a dedicated dining space at home which has all the attributes of a good restaurant and none of the bad (leave the food aside at the moment), then you might find just as much pleasure in staying in and getting the friends to come to you.

Whether you cook for the family or entertain on a regular basis, a well-designed dining space should be on everyone's wish list. It might be a dedicated room or it could be part of the kitchen or lounge, but it is somewhere that you will want to sit, eat, chat, drink and relax. If you have a separate dining room you can indulge any design choices, however, if it is part of another room you need to be clever with the area and you may just resort to dressing the table to create the mood for the meal. It's a tall order for just one space, so how do you tackle it?

STUCK FOR SPACE?

It is frequently the case that you will need to eat in a corner of the kitchen or at one end of the lounge. You will need to choose furniture that fits in the space. This means looking for adaptable tables that can expand to accommodate a group of people and that fold up when they aren't in use so that they don't take up too much space. Whatever style of dining chair that you fancy, make sure that it's one that can stack. Six chairs take up a lot of space if they have to stand alone and will clutter up a room, but if they can be put in a pile you can store them more easily when they aren't needed. They will fit into the space under your stairs or can be tucked into a corner out of the way.

'Few things tend more to alienate friendship than a want of punctuality in our engagements. I have known the breach of a promise to dine or sup to break up more than one intimacy.'
WILLIAM HAZLITT

Defining idea…

If you are looking for ways dress up the space, see IDEA 39, *The essential extras*, on essential accessories

Try another idea…

A DEDICATED ROOM

You can indulge your desire for a very specific look if you have a separate dining room. Whatever the style of the rest of your home, should you wish for ruby red walls, rich velvet-covered seats, a dramatic chandelier and floor-standing candelabras, then here's the space where you can create that look. And boy-oh-boy will you have some parties in there. Without wanting to dampen your enthusiasm for a room that stands alone in the overall scheme of your home, I would suggest that you think about how you are going to prepare the table and present the food. Here's what I am thinking. The room described above will call for gold or silver chargers set beneath the finest china with exquisite glasses for red wine, white wine and water, teamed with fine cutlery and the finest starched table linen. Now if you usually eat from plain white plates, eat with plastic-handled knives and forks and use a handy chunky tumbler for a glass of red wine, these items will not translate into your designer dining room. My point is that you will need to invest in a complete set of glasses, platters, cutlery and serving spoons, mats and all the associated tableware to make such an extravagant scheme work. Do you have the budget to do that or should you work to design a room which will work with items that you already own?

You can treat the preparation of your dining room as putting together a puzzle. The design of the room is the main part of the image and you need all the other pieces in place for it to look complete. Whether you are having a formal dinner to impress the guests or a casual meal for good friends, the same principles apply.

How did it go?

Q   I know all the elements that need to go in, but how do I decide on my scheme?

A   *Well, let's go back to the restaurant theme. Start out by thinking about your favourite one. Is it minimalist and modern with lots of chrome and glass, industrial lighting and chic white china, or is it cosy and dark with rough plaster walls and candles stuffed into Chianti bottles to illuminate the meal? Whatever the elements that make you return time after time, you want to achieve the same effect in your home.*

Q   I have a dining table at the end of my lounge but people always seem to go and sit on the sofa as soon as the meal is over and it breaks up the party. Any solutions?

A   *The real beauty of restaurants is often in the intimacy of the space. It feels right to linger over your coffee and a cigarette. However, at home when you eat at a table positioned at the end of an open-plan lounge, people drift off towards the sofa too quickly once the pudding has been demolished. There is a simple solution. Use a screen to divide the two areas quite clearly into spaces with different functions.*

30

The art of living

From a photograph to a print or a collection of glass to a single much-loved piece of sculpture, you can find a way to display your treasured work of art.

If I ever win the lottery, I will buy an original Elizabeth Frink. I don't want something on the scale of 'Risen Christ' outside Liverpool's Anglican cathedral, but a Goggle Head would be amazing. I'd love to own a Degas bronze — not the ballerinas but a racehorse in motion.

Buying a piece of art is quite an emotive moment. Your choice is such a personal one. And once you get it home and can sit and enjoy your purchase in private it is a thrill that defies any simple explanation. If you think I am getting a bit carried away, just bear with me. I have a limited edition photograph of James Dean that I bought with a whole month's salary in 1987. It would be the first thing that I rescued in a fire. A cast-concrete silver-leafed bowl from a designer whose work I coveted for years, and was finally given as a leaving gift, is a constant inspiration to me. The point of these biographical details is that once I had these pieces, I took some time to decide where and how they would be displayed.

Here's an idea for you...

You may have items in your home that you haven't considered as art but that you can use to make displays. Take glass flower arranging beads for example. Fill two or three plain, straight-sided vases with a variety of different coloured beads and group them together along a windowsill – when the light catches them they look amazing.

What about fairy lights? Wrapped around an empty picture frame and hung on the wall, or curled up inside a big glass bowl and placed in the middle of a shelf they make stylish pieces of 'art'.

Now what we consider as art is a very personal preference, and how we choose to display it comes down to much the same thing. However, there are certain ways to focus attention on a picture or to draw the eye to a much-loved collection that could help when you choose to put these things on display. And the way they are displayed should be sympathetic to the style of the pieces – for example, you can use open-plan shelving for modern collections and lit glass-fronted cabinets for more classical art.

You should take into consideration the following when displaying pieces:

- Wall colour
- Situation
- Lighting

Starting with colour, while most art galleries choose white as the colour against which to hang or display pieces, the walls in your home are likely to be painted or papered in any number of colours. Now you can hang a Mondrian on a wall papered with a stripe but you wouldn't be very happy with the resulting effect it creates. If you have a spectacular picture is it worth considering repainting a recess or chimneybreast in a colour that complements rather than crowds the image? Does the situation show the piece off to its best? A large modern vase calls for space around it so that it can be appreciated without other objects distracting the eye, so maybe you need to consider moving a table into an uncluttered area of the room to allow the art to breathe.

Is there a corner of the room that gets flooded with daylight but then spends the rest of the time in shadow? Your object might look great by day but get lost at night. In which case you should think about getting a light to illuminate the object. If you don't want to start rewiring the room, a lamp moved so that its beam can be directed on the right spot when required is a quick and easy solution to the problem.

Look around your home for a blank wall or empty corner and be open to the idea that a picture destined for the lounge wall might be perfectly placed when hung in the bedroom. Think about moving pieces around and you'll surely end up with the perfect display.

See IDEA 49, *Keep it tidy*, for more information on storage.

Try another idea...

'Without art, the crudeness of reality would make the world unbearable.'
GEORGE BERNARD SHAW

Defining idea...

'The object of art is to give life a shape.'
JEAN ANOUILH, French playwright

Defining idea...

137

How did it go?

Q **Well, I understand how to position a piece, but what sort of prints should I be looking for?**

A *Pick pictures that suit your space. If you live in a loft you'll have large expanses of wall where you can afford to hang huge dramatic canvases. Think about a big Warhol print mounted on a canvas and left unframed. Or go for a dramatic black and white photograph – views from the sky of urban or rural landscapes can look stunning when reproduced on a large scale. For homes decorated in contemporary style, look at graphic prints or hand-printed silkscreen prints. Mount in beech or light wood frames.*

Q **I have looked around and these all seem pretty pricey – any other alternatives?**

A *You'll be amazed at what you can put together without much of a budget. It tends to work out a lot cheaper if you buy a picture and then a frame separately; that way you can shop around for less expensive designs. Take sepia photographs for example. You'll usually find a box full of them at street markets and in the back of antique shops for which you'll pay a few pence. A single picture might have no impact but a line of them across a wall, or a group put together, looks great.*

If you haven't bought a digital camera yet, go out and get one. I know you haven't got much of budget but it could save you a fortune in posters and prints and the possibilities are endless once you can print images from your own computer.

31

Social graces

Get your house dressed up and ready to impress. Have you got one of those friends who you love to visit on a Saturday night? Somehow the house is always welcoming, the lounge looks lovely, the dinner table inviting and if you end up sleeping over, the guest bedroom is a delight.

Your cooking may not always be perfect, but it's more about the ambience that you create when you ask people round to dinner.

And your guest room might double up as a study and have computer equipment and filing cabinets juggling for space with the bed, but it's about making the room welcoming – working around what you have got in place.

Part of getting it right is in the planning. Allow yourself time to prepare the food, tidy the house and get yourself ready. There is nothing worse than the guests arriving in their finery when you haven't had time to get dressed up, never mind that you don't have anywhere to go. It may sound very dull, but a list of jobs and a rough estimate of the time they will take should set you on the right track. Only you know how long you spend on folding eight napkins, laying out eight table settings, getting eight matching glasses together and arranging your flowers. Now that's out of the way, how do your dress up your home?

Here's an idea for you...

Choose a seaside theme for your dinner party and use shells as tealight holders. Make a piece of driftwood into the centrepiece for your table. Go for a Japanese mood and use your coffee table instead of your dining table to eat from. Bring in big floor cushions instead of dining chairs for seats. When you want something rustic, search out those tiny terracotta plant pots, plug the hole in the bottom and use them to hold the pepper and salt.

The finest china, the most elegant linen and some sparkling crystal makes a wonderful setting, but I have found that a few inexpensive 'home-grown' ideas will have guests passing the complements along with the condiments far more effusively. You can make a lovely display even if you are designing on a shoestring. The easiest way is to work within a theme.

TABLE STYLES

If you want to choose a floral theme try some of the following ideas:

- Float a single flower head in a bowl beside each place setting.

- Use brightly coloured tins that held fruit for example and put a posy beside each setting.

- Scatter petals along the length of the table (red roses look amazing against a white cloth).

- Tie a long ribbon around the back of each chair and thread a single stem though each bow.

- Freeze edible flowers in ice cubes so that the drinks match the theme.

There are hundreds of other possibilities but do you get the idea? Think about the theme then write down as many items that are associated with it as possible and see how many of these you can use or adapt to work in the room.

OVERNIGHT STAY

Scent has a powerful effect on people. If your guests walk into their bedroom and there is a wonderful perfume in the air, it immediately says 'welcome'. The subtext is that you have made an effort for them and it makes the room all the more attractive because of that alone. Leave scented candles on the windowsill. With good quality ones, you don't even have to light them because with the heat of the sun, they will give off a scent anyway. Use a fragranced air freshener in the room roughly half an hour before it is going to be used. That way the scent will not be overpowering but will still linger in the air.

If you do have to disguise a work area I would recommend that you buy a folding screen. It may seem like an extravagance for just one night, but this is a versatile piece of furniture that you are investing in. It can go into other rooms and be put to use on other occasions. For hiding clutter there is nothing better.

Entertaining at home should be about both you and your guests being relaxed, so make sure you plan the occasion.

If you are stuck for space to store things in the guest bedroom, see IDEA 42, *It works like a dream*, for some useful hints.

Try another idea...

'Without friends, no one would want to live, even if he had all other goods.'
ARISTOTLE

Defining idea...

'Most women put off entertaining until the kids are grown.'
ERMA BOMBECK, American humorist

Defining idea...

141

How did
it go?

Q   **I'm having a dinner party but while it would be nice to fold up the napkins, I can never seem to get that professional look, all neat and starched. Any tips?**

A   *I know this can be a challenge because it took me a year to perfect the 'table lily'. However, you can just roll up the napkins and use a variety of lovely items as napkin rings to dress them up. Matching up colours can be useful, so if your room is green, tie bear grass around them. If you have a very pretty floral room, use lengths of organza ribbon. For a rustic scene try a length of brown raffia, and if you want to add a bit of glamour, then you can't beat jewel-coloured beads threaded onto fine wire and looped into a ring.*

Q   **OK, I've done that, now what about candlelight. Is it essential?**

A   *Well I would always say 'yes'. It creates an intimacy that overhead lights just can't match. Did you know that if you store your candles in the fridge for a while before lighting them, they will burn for longer? If you don't have enough candlesticks you can use shot glasses to hold them. Also tealights or floating candles placed in a bowl of water tinted with food dye can look amazing.*

32

Things are hotting up

Combine functionality with style when heating your home. Why not have a new hearth custom-made to the exact specifications of your existing design?

You won't have to worry about any gaps between your wood floor and the surround and there will be no need to replace the carpet.

The reason that I bring this up is because quite often we think we are stuck with a fireplace. It seems like an immovable object, but if you want to change your wood surround for marble or your dark hearth for a light stone there's nothing stopping you. The fireplace should be the dramatic focal point of your room, so it needs to be in keeping with your chosen colour scheme and style.

Here's what I suggest. Think of your various heat sources as pieces of furniture. You wouldn't just stick any old sofa in your lounge or any old cabinet in the kitchen – they need to match the mood and the same applies to radiators, fireplaces or stoves. Because there is such a vast array of designs you can match any colour scheme and every style of home.

Here's an idea for you...

If your radiator is positioned on the main wall in a room, think about having it moved. That's usually the place where you want to put the bed in the bedroom or the sofa in the lounge, and with furniture in front of the radiator you will be wasting most of the heat.

...and another...

If you are going to choose a heated towel rail for the bathroom, make sure that you opt for a dual fuel design. These can run off the central heating in the winter, working in tandem with your radiators. They are also wired into the electricity so that in the warmer months you can operate them independently when the heating in the rest of the house is switched off.

FIRESIDE STORIES

If you have inherited a fireplace with a dark slate surround and you want to use a white colour scheme in the room, then switch it for a design in limestone or one of the modern materials that fire manufacturers have developed that allow an amazing amount of detail to be moulded to the design. Ceralite™, for example, developed and copyrighted by Elgin & Hall in the UK, derives its base from limestone rock but is modified in a process that results in it being much sturdier than normal gypsum-based plaster fire surrounds. At the end of the handcrafted manufacturing process, the material has the qualities of a ceramic, and will 'ring' when tapped. (Which will give the party guests something to do as they lean against it with their glass of wine.) I'm not saying that the process of changing a fire is without grief. There will be a lot of mess and dust will get into nooks and crannies that you may not have thought possible to reach. However, the dramatic difference a change of fireplace can make to the room means it has to be considered.

While you are considering this, call in a chimney sweep. Once a year you should have the flue swept to remove soot deposits, to clear old coal and to make sure that it isn't blocked by anything. Birds and their nests can be a problem. If your fire doesn't seem to be burning properly, get the sweep to burn a smoke pellet. This will show whether it is drawing properly and identify cracks in the flue that can be repaired.

There are ways to dress up a plain fireplace and surround. If you are looking for some inspiration, see IDEA 39, *The essential extras.*

Try another idea...

STOVE STYLE

The Swedish know how to do stoves. Their homes often feature grand ceramic designs, tiled or left plain, which can reach from floor to ceiling and make a magnificent feature in a room. If I had a big enough living room and the money to spend, it would be something I would consider choosing.

Stoves can offer the ideal solution if you don't have a fireplace but want some kind of focal point to heat the room. They don't have to be huge or old fashioned and there are designs to run on any type of fuel. Plus you can pick a design with a built-in boiler that will run your radiators and hot water. They are certainly more stylish than the classic white box on the wall type of boiler.

- **Electric**: Plug it in wherever you need a boost – perfect for the conservatory.

- **Gas**: Practical if you can't bear the thought of clearing out a solid fuel design – would suit the bedroom

'Love can bottle the heat in July to warm the chill of December.'
MARGARET GREGSON, author

Defining idea...

'Don't you stay at home of evenings? Don't you love a cushioned seat in a corner, by the fireside, with your slippers on your feet?'
OLIVER WENDELL HOLMES

- **Wood:** Make sure you have a plentiful and reliable source of wood (and only wood can be used) – fit for the kitchen.

- **Multifuel:** Burns smokeless fuel but also wood or even peat – a rustic touch for the lounge.

WALL STORIES

If the most complementary thing you can say about your radiators is that they make somewhere useful to hang the washing, then you really need to get them changed. There is no excuse for living with the classic ugly white designs that you probably inherited with your home. In a modern setting change them for long spring-shaped designs than can run around the room just above skirting board height. Or choose one of the many contemporary shapes available: you can buy a cactus-shaped radiator these days, or if you are looking for something to go in the children's room a design shaped like a big bear. So there's really no excuse for being boring with your choice.

Radiators can also be used as features in a room. Find a design that can also function as a room divider and you combine two elements, heating and design. (That's a good principle to apply to a lot of things in your home – can something fulfil more than one purpose? For example, a screen can be decorative and hide a workstation too. A radiator cabinet can cover an ugly radiator and provide a handy shelf for keys and post in the hall.)

Given the choices in colour and design, there really is no reason why your source of heating can't be as stylish as your curtains, your furniture or your flooring.

Q **According to you the fireplace should be the focal point in the room, but I have a plum sofa and fairly opulent curtains so it doesn't seem to draw the eye.**

How did it go?

A *The simplest solution is to paint the breast above your surround in a colour that contrasts with the surrounding walls. Pick paint that's a slightly darker red than your sofa cover. Also, invest in three tall vases in complementary colours – they should be slightly different heights but make them large. Place one at one end of the mantel and two at the other side. This will help frame the area and draw the eye to the fireplace.*

Q **I've tried that, but the empty fireplace still looks very dull.**

A *I would always recommend putting something in a fireplace when it's not lit. If there isn't a flaming fire to draws the gaze, then make sure there's a pile of logs, a lovely floral display or a decorative fire screen.*

147

33

A piece of the past

Bring classic style to your home with traditional furniture and furnishings. The year in which somewhere was built, the architectural details included in each room and the overall ambience of the place will lead you towards a particular look.

Pick up your house keys and purse and head to Blockbusters or your local multiplex. If your home has a history you'll want to reflect that in your design, and one of the best ways to research a look is to watch a classic movie.

Think about the interiors in Scorsese's *The Age of Innocence* or Merchant Ivory's *The Remains of the Day*. Consider the backdrops in *Dangerous Liaisons* and the sets in *Guess Who's Coming to Dinner*. They all place you right in a particular period from which you can pick out ideas. Clearly museums offer a visual resource too. And there are magazines dedicated to period homes and the way to dress them that offer endless listings of useful stockists and suppliers.

By researching the period you'll be guided towards particular colours, patterns and designs. And while you may want the authenticity that antiques provide, you can use your research to include reproduction pieces that reflect a particular age. Don't

Here's an idea for you... **If you are trying to recreate a period look, remember that designs and styles will have developed over a number of years. The Victorian age, for example, spanned several decades, so allow yourself some flexibility when putting together your room.**

be too rigid in your interpretation unless you want to live in a museum – it could leave you with a 'repressed' room. Stay in sympathy with your chosen style but feel free to allow one or two quirky elements to creep in to create a more relaxed environment.

MAIN FEATURES

You have really lucked out if your house already has particular features that reflect its age. An original fireplace or architectural mouldings like dado or picture rails, wood panelling, cornicing or even a tiled floor could all be the starting point for your design. Can I just say that if you have an original parquet floor then you must lavish it with affection and show it a great deal of love. Treat all of your original gems with respect. Too often people rip them out without due regard for how this will change the face of the place.

But don't despair if you lack these kinds of details, they are easily introduced. Original and reproduction antique fires and mantelpieces can be sourced from manufacturers and reclamation yards. Wood mouldings are simple to fix in place by anyone with even a smidgen of DIY ability and are available in a mix of shapes and styles to suit.

DESIGNER DETAILS

Fabrics have an important role in the period home. Depending on the theme you'll want to look out for sumptuous silk, delicate lace, floral patterned chintzes, heavy damasks or richly coloured velvets. Consider how they were used in the past and you can introduce them today. You could pleat silk and use it as a wall covering for example, a lace panel may make a perfect table runner and a length of velvet might make an ideal throw. The shape of furniture can also influence a mood. Introduce a heavy. imposing mahogany piece for a Victorian-style bedroom or a streamlined sofa in an art deco lounge.

You might want to create a period look by changing the fireplace in your lounge or bedroom. IDEA 32, *Things are hotting up*, might help you make the decision.

Try another idea...

Adding a single choice piece like those above can also create the focus for your room. My advice would be to look out for one purchase that is indicative of the period that you wish to work with and then dress the rest of the room around that. Invest in a chandelier for the lounge, a cheval mirror in the bedroom, an antique washstand in the bathroom or a vintage bedspread in the bedroom.

CHOICES FOR WALLS

'Just build a classic horseshoe of wood and plaster, and fill it with statuary and curtains, then sit back and savor the beautifully blended results.'
MICHAEL WALSH, author

Defining idea...

From Shaker style to art nouveau and from the eighteenth century to the present day, certain colours are associated with certain styles. If you are looking for a guide you'll find period collections available wherever you shop for paint. It's important to get your walls the right shade because they provide the backdrop to the furniture and furnishings that will dress your room. Also don't forget that wallpaper is an option. If the historians who trace its use back to the 1400s are to be believed, then it has most certainly earned a place in the history of home décor.

If you are looking to create a period setting, treasure your original features, supplement them with some reproduction designs, and history shows that you are on the right track.

How did it go?

Q **I've been collecting antique and reproduction pieces for the dining room and have put together my scheme. It has become a bit of an obsession, and I'm wondering if I should continue the look into another room.**

A *You can have one space dressed in period style but, as with any look, if it's not in keeping with the adjacent rooms it can create disharmony in your home. Home design works best when the look is reasonably consistent throughout. If you are going to commit to a period look, you want to consider introducing one or two pieces into other areas but make them background dressing rather than the focal point in the rooms. Make sure that they are complementary to the scheme rather than allowing them to dominate the space – that way they become signposts towards the room that is dedicated to a particular look.*

Q **So you think it's OK to put an antique desk in a contemporary setting?**

A *Every house should have some flexibility to mix and match old and new. Sometimes it is just a matter of making sure that the colours work together and at other times you need to be more blatant about mixing the two styles. If you have a piece of Chinese lacquered furniture, for example, it will sit happily against plain white walls when the floors in the room are made of wood. If your wooden sideboard dates from the nineteenth century perhaps all it needs to make it work in your modern home is for you to dress it up with two or three contemporary vases and some elegant flowers.*

34

That hits the spot

Don't rush the layout of your room. Wouldn't it be perfect if there was a place for everything and everything had its place?

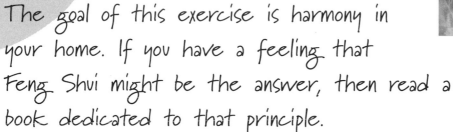

The goal of this exercise is harmony in your home. If you have a feeling that Feng Shui might be the answer, then read a book dedicated to that principle.

I am not in possession of the knowledge to direct you to identify your wealth corner and won't be able to guide you to clear out your relationship area, but I do believe that if you believe in those methods, then they will be beneficial to you. This is a more mundane but still valuable guide to setting up spaces.

THE PERFECT POSITION

Placing furniture can affect the mood of the room and how it is used. The lounge is a good room to use for this exercise.

If you want to create a formal look, keep pieces of furniture square on to each other, chair backs should be flat against walls and tables put at right angles to chairs. Keep coffee table books in carefully stacked piles of two or three diminishing in size from bottom to top.

Here's an idea for you...

Think about the balance of the room. Are all of the larger pieces of furniture on one side of the room and smaller items grouped together on the other? Doesn't just reading that make you feel a little unbalanced? If you can draw an imaginary line across your room from the door to the far wall and position equal sized pieces on either side of the divide it will help to add symmetry to the space.

In contrast, chairs placed at an angle in the corners of rooms, sofas placed to create an L-shape or things displayed at random will seem much more relaxed.

Two large sofas positioned face to face on opposite sides of a large coffee table make it difficult for people to conduct a conversation. A sofa with two armchairs placed at right angles at either end mean a person in each seat will be able to contribute and be heard.

Try this. Draw a floor plan of your room. Try and be accurate with the scaled-down measurements so that you have a realistic idea of how much the chimneybreast sticks out into the space or how much extra floor area there is in the bay window. Remember to put any 'permanent' fixtures like radiators onto the plan and also indicate which way the doors open into the room. Light switches and power points need to be noted so that you don't obstruct them with furniture. Take the plan away with you and sitting somewhere else list all of the furniture that is currently in the room. Beside each piece put down its function (seating for chairs, lighting for lamps, storage for bookcases, etc.)

Now think about how you use the room and assess whether you need every piece that is in there or whether there is something missing that would make the room work more efficiently. Think about whether the coffee table is actually in the wrong place for people to reach it with ease when they are sitting on the sofa. Or is a lamp positioned so far away from a reading chair that it can't possible function as a task light? These are just some of the things that you can easily change.

I am a fan of open, airy spaces. So I would also recommend that you decide if you really need every piece of furniture in the room. Could one of the three bookshelves be moved to the hallway? Would it be possible to take out the second armchair and still have enough seating for everyday use? There is nothing better than imagining a room with nothing in it and then mentally placing the pieces on your list in one by one according to the importance of their function in the room. (A sofa is the most important piece in the lounge, a bed the most vital item in the bedroom.) As you work down your list you may realise that a writing desk would function just as easily in the dining room as the lounge and by removing it you would be uncluttering a crowded corner.

Look at IDEA 49, *Keep it tidy*, if you are worried about your storage solutions

Try another idea...

'I have been black and blue in some spot, somewhere, almost all my life from too intimate contacts with my own furniture.'
FRANK LLOYD WRIGHT

Defining idea...

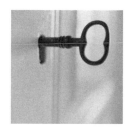 

Here are some things to consider when you are planning other rooms...

■ **Hallway:** Does the table you have put beside the front door make it difficult to negotiate the space and would a wall-mounted narrow shelf provide an alternative solution?

■ **Bedroom:** Is all the storage that you have in there essential or could a dressy cupboard be positioned on the landing in a recess at the top of the stairs? (Remember that you have to allow space for the sweep of the opening doors.)

■ **Dining room:** Would you be better to get rid of two half-height cabinets and replace them with a taller unit that will house the contents of both but free up floor space, somewhere that you can stack chairs when you take the leaves out of the extending table, for example?

Plan the layout of your room with care and you'll find it both pleasurable and practical to use.

Defining idea...

'Plans are nothing; planning is everything.'
DWIGHT D. EISENHOWER

Q   Well, I have drawn the plan but I can't see how I can remove any of the pieces in the room as they all serve a purpose.

A   OK, but can they be put to that purpose in another space? We are back with the wardrobe on the landing which can house clothes that don't need to be accessible every day – formal dresses, coats, winter shoes in the summer months for example. You might also want to go through a decluttering exercise (see IDEA 15, Keep it tidy) as it could be that you can get rid of things and so reduce the amount of storage that you really need.

Q   But what if I am still left with the same amount of furniture?

A   Planning a space should also include thinking about alternatives to the items that you already have in place. So while you may currently need a cabinet for the television, is it possible that you could be investing in a wall-mounted flat screen design at some point? And while the freestanding bookshelves seem essential in your study, would it be better in the long term to get some custom-built shelves put into the alcoves at either side of the door where currently the space is wasted?

How did it go?

35

Left on the shelf

**Choosing and using the simplest of storage solutions. How
many? How deep? How high? It is impossible to live
without a shelf somewhere in your house.**

There, I have laid down the challenge
for someone to prove me wrong, but I say the
more shelves the merrier.

When you consider that everyone has something that needs a home, and everyone
has the desire to store certain items where they can not only see them but also
easily reach them, then shelving is a logical solution.

This is the shelving chapter – you might think it crosses over with storage, and
you'd be right. I'm not talking about cabinets – just simple shelves. If this seems a
bit polarized look at the following issues which you need to consider when
planning your shelves:

- Built-in or freestanding?
- Glass or wood?
- Suspended in space or with obvious supports?
- Deep enough for books or slim enough to suit CDs and DVDs?
- Long enough to stretch across an entire wall?
- Short so that they make a feature on their own?

Do you have a room that is chock-a-block with furniture? Work out how much floor space is taken up by cabinets and cupboards. Then assess the contents of these pieces of furniture and consider whether they would fit on wall-mounted shelves. (Do a quick decluttering exercise while you consider this.) The amount of wasted wall space in any home is immense. The number of rooms that would benefit in terms of looks and ease of use if some floor space was freed up is just as great. So put the two together and the solution is to put up some shelves.

Defining idea...

'Life has a way of setting things in order and leaving them be. Very tidy, is life.'
JEAN ANOUILH, French playwright

Whether you opt for built-in or freestanding is as much to do with the layout and design of your home as your personal preferences. If you live in an older property with architectural features, the natural place for built-in shelves is the alcove either side of a chimneybreast. But in a more modern home, there are still areas that can be used. Think about the area above doors and the space underneath a staircase. These can be fitted with shelves or provide somewhere to introduce a freestanding unit. Now a thought about materials. One of the finest makeshift shelving systems I have seen was in a student flat. Financially challenged but needing some storage, they had used breezeblocks and glass to create a set of shelves. The pleasing contrast of stone and glass gave them a designer air, and because the glass wasn't too long and the breezeblocks were very sturdy, they were an example of the safest form of shelving – where the shelves aren't too long to support their load and the supports are strong enough to withstand a few knocks. Wood shelves are all well and good – practical and easy to buy 'off the shelf', as it were. However, it's important to think about alternatives and that is where glass comes in. If you wish to display a particular piece, then glass has the advantage that you can shine light on the object of your affections from below.

In the kitchen it may fit in with your style to put up a slatted metal shelf, something that will fit in with an industrial look. The advantage to this kind of shelf is that you can also hang butcher's hooks from the underside, which increases the number of storage solutions that they offer.

Other issues that relate to shelving can be easily resolved. Measure the depth of your biggest books for the shelves in the library. Work out how much space your kitchen equipment – with all necessary attachments and accessories – will take up. Consider whether you have enough floor area in the bathroom for a freestanding set of shelves or whether you are going to have to settle for a space-saving solution.

Above all, it takes an honest assessment of the objects that are going to live there so be realistic about how much room they will need when you plan for your shelves.

If you are wondering if you missed a storage opportunity, take a look at IDEA 47, *Have you wasted that loft space?*

Try another idea...

'*As the biggest library if it is in disorder is not as useful as a small but well-arranged one, so you may accumulate a vast amount of knowledge but it will be of far less value than a much smaller amount if you have not thought it over for yourself.*'
ARTHUR SCHOPENHAUER

Defining idea...

How did it go?

Q Are you saying that I should get rid of all my cabinets? Surely there are certain things that are better hidden behind closed doors.

A   Not at all. I agree that if you are a clutter queen then you need to be able to hide lots of rubbish where it won't become an eyesore. But you would be amazed at how good even the most basic of things can look if you make the effort to put them on display; a set of white china can be appealing in a dining room; a collection of jugs in all shapes, sizes and colours will look wonderful in the kitchen, and on a practical note, information stored in stylish box files is more easily accessible when all you have to do is reach up to a shelf and not go rummaging in a cupboard.

Q But shelves are all basically the same shape, which is pretty dull.

A   Again, not at all. There is a classic design to look out for which is a piece of curling wood that makes a shelf. I have seen a luggage rack from a train used as a place for pots and pans to live. You can use wire or wicker baskets in a run as a kind of shelving system, and don't forget that corbels make neat shelves for positioning a candle or a small vase.

36

Softly, softly

Weave a mix of materials into the fabric of your home. Whether you are a fan of patterns or like to keep things plain, the fabrics that you choose to use play a huge part in developing the style of your home.

The soft side of any home encompasses a great range of items: upholstery, curtains, throws, blinds and bed linen to cover just a few. Now there are certain fabrics that will be ideal for certain jobs and others that are so versatile that you can put them just about anywhere.

Light linens will make super curtains but are not good for upholstering chairs that will get a lot of wear and tear; velvets are ideal for upholstering pieces but don't make up into good loose covers.

The most important role of fabric is to bring colour and comfort into a room. If you imagine a space decorated in plain neutral shades, then the inclusion of a blind in a contrasting colour adds interest to the room. If you think about a bedroom that is predominantly dressed in cool colours, then a fluffy chenille throw on the bed introduces a cosy touch.

163

Here's an idea for you...

When you come to dress your windows, don't just think curtains or blinds – you can use all sorts of different lengths of fabrics there. In a room decorated along exotic lines, a sari might be the perfect window covering. If you are creating a cosy country cottage mood, how about using a blanket? Little clip hooks that run along curtain poles to which you attach the fabric mean you can dress your windows even if you have no sewing skills at all.

Let's approach this by looking at some rooms. There may be places where you can use fabric that you hadn't considered, for example in the bedroom. Is your headboard hard wood or iron? Would a padded or fabric-covered headboard be a better option if you love to sit in bed and watch TV or read? I don't mean that you necessarily have to have a fitted, frilled and pleated design – very country house hotel – you can have a reasonably plain one. A large oblong of fabric that you simply fold over the headboard and tie in place has the advantage that you can take it off to wash it. Still looking at the bed, if you have invested in underbed storage, would the addition of a valance make the set-up look more attractive? Once again, you don't need to have frills. A neat kick-pleat valance sits flat all the way around the bed – it looks smart rather than flamboyant and if made to match the headboard brings a scheme neatly together.

Dressing the bed offers a perfect opportunity for introducing stacks of lovely fabrics. Although most of us use duvets, there is something wonderful about getting into a bed that has been made up with sheets, blankets and an eiderdown or bedspread. Of course you can layer these on top of a duvet too but for the sake of neatness make sure that the various layers are large enough to completely cover the edges of the duvet beneath. Layering with fabric like this means you can have some fun with colours and patterns. Combine plain fabrics with chintz and checks. Use stripes with ginghams and simple florals – make sure that the colours match and you can introduce all sorts of different designs to the bed. And never forget to pile it up with lots of lovely cushions in addition to your pillows.

If you are thinking about underbed bedroom storage, see IDEA 42, It works like a dream.

Try another idea...

The lounge is home to all sorts of items that will need to be dressed with fabric: chairs and sofas, pouffes and footstools and of course the windows. When you are thinking about the fabrics for this room, remember that one of the functions of fabrics can be to bring different textures into a space. Imagine that you are having loose cotton covers on your sofa – you might choose a damask to upholster an armchair that will sit beside the sofa and a heavy velvet or suede for the footstool. You could then pick heavy linen for your curtains or blinds. It's quite astonishing how much of an impact this can create. On a simpler scale, just draping a woollen throw over the back of a chair adds interest to the space.

'We live in a web of ideas, a fabric of our own making.'
JOSEPH CHILTON PEARCE, scholar and scientist

Defining idea...

Another room where fabrics can be used for visual impact is the dining room. If you think about the combination of a tablecloth, napkins, upholstered seats, table runners and again the window treatments, there are plenty of places to play with different patterns within your chosen colour scheme.

If you have a designer wood or glass tabletop that you wish to show off, then use a table runner in place of a tablecloth. The contrast of, say, a washed white wood table and a green checked runner bordered with a floral fabric is pleasing to the eye.

'Man never made any material as resilient as the human spirit.'
BERN WILLIAMS, author

Defining idea...

Remember that the comfort of your guests is important when they sit down to eat, so if your chairs have hard seats think about having some padded tie-on cushions made to match your runner – it's a neat way to pull a scheme together.

How did it go?

Q I am thinking about combining a blind and curtain at a window. Should I go for contrasting colours or is it more important to make sure that the texture of the fabrics is different?

A *I would opt for colour contrast first. For example, a taupe linen blind can sit happily behind cream linen curtains but if you were to mix cotton and velvet it might look a little strange. There are certain combinations that can work, voiles teamed with cotton for example, but first get as large a piece of fabric as you can for the two different jobs and lay them together to see if the textures work.*

Q Are there any recommendations for which tiebacks to team with particular fabrics?

A *Unless you are going to have them made up in the same fabric as the curtains, then use your tiebacks to add a touch of contrast. I would put traditional coloured cord tiebacks with fringed tassels in classic settings where the curtains are made in heavy chintz and opt for something more casual like rope if you have used cotton or linen for your drapes.*

37

An informal affair

Why should you choose an unfitted, freestanding kitchen? If you have a large enough room, then the freedom of a freestanding design is very hard to beat.

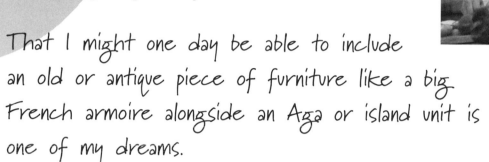

That I might one day be able to include an old or antique piece of furniture like a big French armoire alongside an Aga or island unit is one of my dreams.

This is part of the appeal of such rooms – that everything in the space doesn't have to match perfectly. There might be modern items alongside more traditional pieces, and you might have pine mixed with oak or chrome mixed with wood. Another advantage to this type of kitchen is that if you are vertically challenged you can buy pieces which are at the perfect practical height for you. Now of course it is possible with a hand-built fitted kitchen to get your work surface put in at any height, however designs bought off the peg are usually standard heights – not designed for those of us with shorter legs.

I would say at this point that you must have a room of generous proportions to be able to get away with a freestanding kitchen. All the elements will take up much more floor space than a fitted design. But if you do have such a luxury, then you can really enjoy putting together a room over a period of time. Put the basics in – your

Here's an idea for you...

In a freestanding kitchen you must be aware that your work surfaces could be more fragmented than in a fitted room. On the one hand this means you need to carefully consider just how much surface room you need, and on the other it gives you the perfect opportunity to pick more expensive materials for the smaller spaces. Corian is a wonderfully practical material but pricey, and granite is wonderful in a kitchen but again at a much higher price than laminate designs. In general, stone and solid surfaces make the most expensive choices while wood is just ahead of laminate.

cooker, fridge, sink, etc. – but then rummage around for junk buys to complement your room and allow the scheme to grow over months or years.

If you are already falling in love with this idea, it may be worth getting in a builder or kitchen designer at this point. This is because with freestanding kitchens you may need to reroute plumbing, gas or electricity supplies depending on where you are going to position your sink, dishwasher and cooker – it is possible to have a lovely contemporary cooker hood hanging from the ceiling in the middle of the room, but you would be advised to get an idea of the costs involved before getting too carried away with your ideas for an island hob with griddle on one side.

There are certain things to bear in mind when putting together your floor plan for the room: foremost is that you need space around each item in the room. Try to visualise the different areas that you are going to need – the preparation area, the cooking space, the storage area and, if the room is large enough, the eating and seating area too. There is something very appealing about a kitchen with a lovely worn sofa stuck in one corner – somewhere usually for the dogs to sleep! Now while all of the above may require specific spaces, in certain cases they can be moved around. I am talking about introducing a portable island that will offer you more flexibility than a built-in design. A butcher's block on wheels can be moved to the sink when you are chopping vegetables so

Read IDEA 25, *A professional opinion*, before you bring in your builder.

Try another idea...

that you can rinse and chop in the same area, and then it can be wheeled over to the cooker when you want to start making the meal. There is another advantage, which is that it makes it much easier to clean the floor when you can move a trolley out of the way while you mop.

In a kitchen where the walls will not be covered with cupboards, you need to consider what type of splashback you require on the walls. It's clearly vital around the cooking and

'*If you can organize your kitchen, you can organize your life.*'
LOUIS PARRISH, author

Defining idea...

food preparation areas, so what are your choices? Stainless steel will fit with a modern kitchen and you can buy ready-made panels to fit behind the cooker, while glass allows you to see through to the surface behind so would be perfect if there is a paint effect on your walls. Tiles are the norm and within everyone's budget, but if you have the cash splash out on granite for a stunning effect when combined with a work surface in the same material. Laminate designs will offer you a wide range of colour options if you are looking to stick with one particular colour in your room.

So you can see the appeal of putting together a freestanding kitchen. Now start searching out lots of lovely furniture for your room.

Q **Without fitted cabinets, under which or inside of which I can put lights, how do I tackle the lighting scheme in a freestanding kitchen?**

A *I would always favour recessed spotlights, but make sure you don't put them all on the same circuit. For example, have one set specifically positioned to illuminate the preparation and cooking areas in the room. Have another set that illuminates the dining area or if you are lucky enough to room for a sofa, then the seating area. Make sure that both sets are on dimmer switches.*

Q **No pendant lights then?**

A *Are you thinking about having a hob with extractor fan positioned in the middle of the room? Is one of the ways you are going to increase storage by having a hanging rack for saucepans suspended from the ceiling? If so you can see why it would be better to avoid pendant lights as the fittings may well jostle for space. It's much better to keep the ceiling clear of any other clutter.*

38

Lounging around

Design your living room for each and every situation. Disagree with me if you wish, but I would maintain that your lounge is the hardest working room in the house.

Morning, noon and night it has to be available for watching TV, reading, snoozing, entertaining and eating. When somewhere is on call for all of these activities there is a long list of requirements, but combining comfort with practicality is a must.

If you put together the 'near as perfect as you can' living room, you have achieved a level of success in interior design for which you can be truly proud. It means that you have understood the principles of laying out a room, embraced the idea that a space works on many levels, and made no mistake in choosing furniture to fulfil a whole range of requirements.

Let's start with seating. Supplement your sofa with one or two armchairs so that should you wish to sprawl out, then everyone else can relax too. If you bring in a pouffe and some floor cushions other people can put their feet up or relax on the

Here's an idea for you...

Be prepared to rearrange the furniture to make better use of the space. You may be wedded to the idea that the sofa should be the place that you sit when you want to watch TV, but is it possible that if you shift it to a different part of the room it will serve more than that one purpose? Could it be repositioned so that when every seat is occupied it makes it easier to chat? Would it make sense to move it from in front of the radiator so that you are heating the room more efficiently?

floor. Look through any contemporary mail order catalogue and you'll find wool-, felt- and suede-covered stools that are a far cry from the designs available to our parents' generation. While you are flipping through the pages keep an eye out for beanbags. Of course now that they are made in leather they are no longer called 'beanbags' but have been tagged with the far more sophisticated label of 'floor seats'. Whatever. They can still be chucked at the person who complains that there is nowhere to sit.

Now, what about reading and watching the television? You might be thinking that they require nothing special, but have you got your lights positioned so that there is no glare on the screen and so that you aren't going to strain your eyes. A lamp that can be moved around to accommodate your activities is an essential piece of kit in the lounge. Without it you have to rely on overhead or wall lights and these can seldom be positioned perfectly to suit every activity.

Next, have you got a table close to hand? Whether it's a coffee table that stays in one place or part of a nest of three that you pull out and use according to your needs, you want somewhere that you can set down the remote control or pile up the numerous sections of the weekend papers, not to forget an easy-to-reach surface for a cup of tea (daytime) or a glass of wine (after 5 o'clock).

By the way, a nest of tables sounds horribly old fashioned but designs in maple, glass with alloy and acrylic make them suitable for modern homes.

If you want to dress up the space, see IDEA 39, *The essential extras.*

Try another idea...

Any space that accommodates all of these activities also has a responsibility to cope with the associated flotsam and jetsam. There will be books that need a home and videos or DVDs that you have got to store somewhere. If you have a stereo in the room, then you can't just leave CDs littering any available flat surface.

'Television is like the invention of indoor plumbing. It didn't change people's habits. It just kept them inside the house.'
ALFRED HITCHCOCK

Defining idea...

This is the ideal opportunity to make use of any area that has been created by the construction of your home. If you have a space either side of a chimneybreast, for example, then put it to use as the perfect place for housing custom-built shelving. A recess created by the positioning of a dividing wall can serve the same purpose. Alternatively, buy a freestanding unit but make sure that you can adjust the height of the shelves. There is nothing more frustrating than a bookcase where every single shelf is positioned at a uniform height. It means a lot of wasted space when you are using it to house a range of books, magazines and videos all of which have different dimensions.

Designing a practical lounge takes some amount of planning, but once the pieces are in place you'll be glad that you spent the time getting it right.

'The time to relax is when you don't have time for it.'
SYDNEY J. HARRIS, American journalist

Defining idea...

How did it go?

Q   **I have brought in storage and moved the furniture around but every activity seems to call for a different layout. It's not practical to constantly move the furniture around so what do I do?**

A   *Prioritise. Do you mostly entertain, watch TV or relax and read a book? Is this space the kid's playroom as well as your lounge? Set up the room to fit with its primary function and then create other spaces in your home. Put a sofa in the bedroom so that you can stretch out and read in there. Make the kitchen somewhere that you sit around a table to entertain. Clear out the box room and make it into a den for the children so that they have a space that they can call their own.*

Q   **Right I've done that and decided that my priority is entertaining. Which piece of furniture belongs where?**

A   *Create areas in the room that are conducive to different uses. Put two sofas or a sofa and chair at right angles to each other so that people can sit down and chat within hearing distance of each other. Make sure that you position a side table between two armchairs so that the people who don't wish to settle into a long conversation can sit for a minute but leave their glasses behind when they wish to move on. Also if there is one perfect place to stand with a glass and observe what is going on around you, it's against the mantel around a fire, so don't clutter up that area with a table or chair. Leave the floor clear for people to lean.*

39

The essential extras

Add the finishing touch to any space with a few fundamental pieces.

After the decoration is done and all of the furniture has been positioned in the perfect place, your room will need titivating. This is the technical term for those final touches that give a scheme life and interest.

They are the bits and pieces that can be collected over time, added to with holiday mementoes, wedding gifts and an occasional collector's piece. They might be a chance buy or a carefully chosen and saved-up-for design classic, but whatever their provenance their job is to dress up a space. Let me explain it like this – think of these items like fashion accessories. You've got your your basic outfit; then you add jewellery, shoes, a belt or a scarf to complete the look. In terms of your home these translate into mirrors, vases, cushions, throws, bowls, pictures, frames and clocks.

Sometimes you need to add a focal point to a room. These 'essentials' can perform this role and a larger-than-life accessory may do the job. If you have ever walked into a restaurant and seen a huge clock on an otherwise bare wall, you'll appreciate how it can grab the attention. My kitchen is a plain oblong shape with no

Here's an idea for you...

You can never have too many vases. Vases are one of those items that when put in a collection can become like still-life works of art. Imagine gathering together different shaped designs but all in shades of cream. Group them on a side table in the corner of a room and they draw the eye and give that area of the room a purpose, where previously it was just an unexciting space for the table. Start collecting glass designs in various different shades – in this case it is the material that unifies the collection rather than the colour. Whether you favour huge floral displays or prefer the minimalist approach of one or two stems in a run of two or three matching vases, they offer an easy way to add an injection of colour to a room, dressing it up before your very eyes.

architectural details or decorative effects to draw the eye. I have positioned a large clock on the bare wall that faces you as you walk into the room. It adds a touch of drama to the space.

There isn't a room in the house that won't be improved by the introduction of a mirror, and the bigger the better as far as I am concerned. If you are choosing one for the bedroom make sure that it is tall enough to give a full head-to-toe reflection. This might mean investing in a cheval-style design which comes complete with legs and is more like a piece of furniture than an accessory. Or it might mean that you simply stand the design on the floor rather than mount it on the wall. (Don't worry that this might appear to the untrained eye like you haven't bothered to get out your drill and screws, this look is very much in vogue.) Just make sure that the mirror is also wide enough to lean without falling over. Mirrors can be used to bounce light into dark corners and create an illusion of space in a small rooms – they are a must-have accessory.

There are lots of pieces that taken one by one perform different jobs in a room. Let's take cushions as another essential accessory and one that can be used to bring comfort and colour to a room. Now everyone is familiar with a standard square design and these are all well and good. However, I would urge you to try and mix in some different shapes and sizes. Place a large continental cushion behind a couple of the classic size when you are dressing your sofa. Include one or two bolster cushions with the pillows on your bed. Look for oblong designs and tiny squares and mix them all together. Also choose designs with different trimmings and edgings – look for some with tasselled edges, some with fabric-covered fastening buttons and one or two with mother of pearl or wooden toggles. By mixing up these different elements you are adding lots of interest to the space in which they are placed.

Remember that every room will benefit from a little dressing up and enjoy working on this, the last stage, in putting together your scheme.

See IDEA 30, *The art of living*, for more ideas on displaying items.

Try another idea...

'A flowerless room is a soulless room, to my way of thinking; but even one solitary little vase of a living flower may redeem it.'
VITA SACKVILLE-WEST

Defining idea...

'It is the unseen, unforgettable, ultimate accessory of fashion that heralds your arrival and prolongs your departure.'
COCO CHANEL

Defining idea...

How did it go?

Q   **This all sounds lovely, but if I go out and buy lots of accessories it's going to cost a fortune!**

A   *OK, if everything was supposed to be brought into the room at the same time it might. However part of the fun of accessorising a room is to introduce pieces over time. A rummage in an antique shop might produce a lovely old clock. A trip to your local junk shop might result in you finding a slightly worn (but all the more attractive for that) mirror. The idea is to accumulate your collection over time.*

Q   **But I need some accessories *now* to dress up the room.**

A   *Please try to think a bit laterally. In the case of vases, for example, have a look around your home for other items that can be used in a floral display. Jugs are the obvious one but do you have an old metal kettle or an unused china teapot? Have you got any designer water bottles or wine carafes that can be brought into service for this job? Remember that the item itself doesn't have to be inherently waterproof. You can place a plastic bag full of water inside an object so that the flowers can drink. How about using an upturned straw hat or a handbag to create an unusual display?*

40

Small but perfectly formed

Simple solutions for pocket-sized spaces. With clever use of colour and careful planning, even the smallest space works as a fully functioning home.

If it's true that our possessions expand to fill the available space, then give me a studio flat every time. Not an expansive loft-style studio but a well-designed and compact home.

It has to be said that if you are hopelessly untidy then you are going to have to work harder at this than if you were born with that elusive neat and tidy gene.

However, there is something very appealing about a space that works as a kitchen to cook in, a dining room to eat in and a bedroom to sleep in. It presents a challenge whether you are a slob or impeccably neat. How do you divide the different areas to define the disparate uses? How do you maximise the look of the space while creating different zones?

That's studio living. But what about a house conversion where each floor of the building was originally designed as one-third of a functioning home and is now divided into three separate units where the rooms seem very small?

Here's an idea for you...

You can use light, both natural and from fixtures and fittings, to manipulate space. In a small room, make sure that your window treatment doesn't obscure any of the window – you need to let as much sunshine in as possible. If part of your home is in the roof, keep the skylights clean and clear. One useful tip in small spaces is to use lights at floor level to lead the eye. Spotlights installed just above the skirting and running away from a kitchen area and towards the lounge will draw the eye away from the kitchen if you have extinguished all the lights in that area.

For both situations, let's start with an illusion. In any situation where your floor space is limited you need to decorate and design it so that the area seems larger than it is. In the first place, choose a light colour to paint your walls. In the second place choose a light colour to decorate your ceiling. In the third place choose a light-coloured flooring. (You will bring in other details later so that this isn't as bland as it sounds.)

Now let's be realistic. You can't have a massive sofa, you can't have a king-sized bed. Apart from the style issues that need to be considered, they probably won't go up the stairs or get through the door. In the same way that a doll's house has pieces that are miniaturised versions of the real thing, you are going to have to sit on a diminutive sofa and sleep in a moderately sized bed. (If you can't bear the thought of that, a wall bed might be the answer; a design that folds away can be huge because it won't take up floor space when shut away.)

Just as a jug can also function as a vase and a mug might be the place where you keep your pens and pencils, so when you buy furniture for small spaces work on the principle that, where possible, you want to get two uses out of one item. A coffee table doubles up as a dining table if you have floor cushions to sit on while you eat, a storage chest functions as extra seating when covered with lovely blankets or throws, and a set of shelves can also become a room divider. Once you start to work on this principle you'll find your own ways to adapt things in your home.

If you are struggling as to how to lay out your rooms, see IDEA 34, *That hits the spot*, for some guidance.

Try another idea...

Colour is a useful tool in defining spaces. Variations on the walls and in the floor can be a great way to signpost a change of use. While I have said, and stick to the idea, that everything should be kept light, you can still use a slightly darker paint in two different spaces. If your kitchen is pure white, then decorate the adjacent designated dining area in a shade of stone. And you can change the flooring – if the lounge area in a studio is covered in wood laminate, then choose seagrass to cover the space that you use as a study.

I would also urge you to consider investing in vertical blinds or sliding panels to screen off spaces. These can be fitted to run from floor to ceiling and are easily pulled out of the way when you want to be open plan, and drawn back into place when you wish to separate off your sleeping area for example.

(Just another quick note about decorating – your use of patterns should ideally be kept to a minimum in small spaces. I'm afraid you would be unwise to use a boldly patterned wallpaper even if you have fallen in love with the current trend for retro-style bold designs that seem to be used in every designer home in the magazines.) Much as I hate to state the obvious, storage will be a priority in your compact home. You need to take an uncluttered approach to living in any small space so have a good look around your home and pinpoint any areas that are completely clear. You can look at the floor for starters but then include the walls all the way up to the ceiling too. There is an area above every doorway that can be used to house a set of shelves. You'll find space beneath each set

'Room service? Send up a larger room.'
GROUCHO MARX

Defining idea...

181

of stairs that might be ideal for hanging hooks. Invest in clothes bags that fit under the bed in the bedroom, inset a basin into a cabinet in the bathroom and use the plinth space in your kitchen for extra drawers, and you'll be well on the way to making the most of any dead space.

How did it go?

Q   I don't want to start messing about with the existing lights in my studio. What are my options?

A   *I would recommend investing in two or three lamps in a range of heights. If you have the ability to direct beams into different areas of the room you can create different focal points depending on which space you are using. Remember to turn off ceiling or wall lights in any area that you are not using and use the lamps to illuminate the space that you are currently occupying. Point one up towards the top of the wall to wash it in light and focus another on a particular item in the space, be it a picture, a table or a chair.*

Q   But doesn't that mean I'm going to have to keep moving the lamps around?

A   *Well yes, but that's why they are lamps – the idea is that they are portable, not fixed lights. You have to be flexible in small spaces. If you can't bear the idea that you will have to unplug them and trail flexes around, then it is possible to buy little lights that are battery powered and can be easily stuck in place. Of course you will need to position them so that you can easily replace the battery but it might be one solution. Also never forget the power of candlelight. A group of candles lit at one end of a darkened space will immediately draw the eye into that area.*

41

The soft side

Floors that feel supple underfoot. Kick off your shoes and take a walk. Cushion each step with a covering that keeps your feet warm and that cuts down on noise.

Take a walk on the natural side or vote with your feet for vinyl. If you are into that kind of thing, run your feet over rubber just for the thrill of it. There's no reason to not mix your choice of flooring throughout your home and the soft options are vast and very versatile.

If you are tempted to dismiss all natural floorings as just grass, then you need to take a closer look. Each type has different qualities that you will come to appreciate over time, and surprisingly, paper is in this category too. While it may not be the first type of material that you consider for your floors, it's now very much part of this popular group. It's woven into a durable flooring material and the addition of resin to the mix increases its resistance to moisture.

Coir is the tough face of this family and makes a great choice for hardworking areas such as the hall. It may be a little rougher underfoot than the rest but practically it

Here's an idea for you...

Make sure that you clean all these floors in the proper way. For example, water and coir *do not mix*. You need to make sure with many soft types of flooring that they have been treated with a stain resistor, then you just need to vacuum regularly. Laminate, cork and vinyl can all be treated in much the same way. First vacuum, then go over the surface with a damp (not sopping) mop.

makes a lot of sense. If you are looking for a more sensitive option here's a tip: jute makes the ideal choice for bedrooms because it is much softer underfoot, though of course much less durable to traffic. Somewhere in between these two in terms of comfort sits sisal, so that may suit your dining room or lounge. Seagrass works happily in most spaces because it is smooth in texture but tough on the ground.

(Just a quick note for those who love to research, in depth, items for their home. Natural flooring comes from places as diverse as Brazil and Africa, Bangladesh, India and China, and it makes fascinating reading when you look into the various sources and manufacturing of these types of flooring.)

Vinyl may have an image problem but do give it a second thought. It's durable, it's washable and it offers comfort underfoot. Another plus is that there is such a wide range of colours and designs available that if you have inherited a room where you are quite happy with the décor but need to change the flooring, you are bound to find a colour match for the existing scheme. Top quality vinyl reproduces the look of stone and tiles, and there are some wood finishes that would defy the most rigorous comparison with the real thing (albeit from a distance of about 10 metres).

Linoleum is very different from vinyl although the two are often grouped together. The former is a natural product while the latter comes from synthetic materials. As with many natural materials lino improves, if cared for properly, with age. And it is a good choice if you are asthmatic as it won't attract dust and dust mites.

Rubber and **cork** are both soft options. Rubber is resilient, water resistant and it's available in some amazing colours too. If you want it, patterns can be part of the make-up with grooves, squares, circles and studs all available. If you want a scarlet floor in the bathroom, this is the material to look at. If you are planning a modern kitchen and are unsure of which flooring to choose, this would be perfect for the job.

Cork can be dyed, so you would have the option of a coloured floor, but the reason to settle on this is for its softness and soundproofing qualities.

You may want to consider a different type of floor. See IDEA 28, *A tough decision*, and IDEA 48, *A night on the tiles*, for other floor options.

Try another idea...

'*My kitchen linoleum is so black and shiny that I waltz while I wait for the kettle to boil. This pleasure is for the old who live alone.*'
FLORIDA SCOTT-MAXWELL, American writer

Defining idea...

185

How did
it go?

Q   **So which natural flooring would be best for an older home?**

A   *Because of the range of textures and colours available, you can find a design for both modern and traditional interiors. If you look at historical buildings you'll often see grass mats used to cover floors, but because we live in modern times I think you should consider the use of the room over and above the material. Remember that all flooring should be able to withstand the wear and tear it will receive. Having said that, the roughest type of coir will suit a rustic setting, while the finest sisal would be better for a more formal room.*

Q   **If I want to use vinyl flooring should I opt for tiles or buy it on a roll?**

A   *This is a consideration for many types of flooring. One simple way of making your choice is to consider the size of the room that you are working with. Any flooring sold in sheet form gives you a lovely seamless finish which is ideal for a large area. Where there is little floor space and you have to fit the flooring around lots of recesses or cabinets that project into the room, tiles might be a better choice as they can be cut to fit perfectly.*

42

It works like a dream

Sensible storage solutions for the bedroom are a must. You know those mini-mail order catalogues that drop out of the middle of your magazine?

They are filled with miracle cleaning products, mug trees, scented drawer liners and an assortment of gadgets that you never knew you needed, or even thought existed. You flick through them wondering who buys a miniature cabinet for keys or a mitt for removing fluff from clothes. But every now and then you spot a gem of an idea.

Next time you get such a catalogue don't just bin it but see if you can spot plastic bags that you fill with clothes or bed linen then attach to the nozzle of your vacuum cleaner to suck all the excess air out of the bag. They don't rate in the looks department, but what a great way to reduce the amount of space you need for storage. When summer comes and you are putting away your winter wardrobe you could store it in a fraction of the space it would normally take up. Now that we've

Here's an idea for you... **Before you buy furniture for the bedroom decide on the position of your bed. Does positioning it against one wall mean you have a wasted area behind the door? If you want it under the window are you going to lose the use of a recess that could be made into a seat with a space for storage beneath? Work with the architectural features of the room so that no area becomes a dead space.**

shared that neat idea we can address other storage issues in the bedroom.

It must be every woman's idea of heaven to have a walk-in closet or room dedicated to the storage of clothes. Imagine how easy it would be to organise your jackets, jumpers, suits and shoes if there was a room set aside with stacks of racks and rails all dedicated to that one purpose. No bed to climb over, no dressing table to walk around, just a clear run of outfits. Joy. It's a fact of life that very few of us have enough space in our homes to accommodate such luxury (but if you do, lucky you).

So what are the alternatives? Put aside any prejudices you have against built-in wardrobes. The image of awful white or cream plastic-looking fronts is outdated, and chic modern designs offer mirrored units that don't look like they belong in a 70s porn movie. They are not everyone's cup of tea and don't suit every style of room, but because they can be built to accommodate sloping ceilings, awkward recesses and changes in the floor level they make efficient use of the space that they take up.

What's the first thing you do when you get home after a shoe-shopping spree? Pull open the boxes, chuck them aside and try on your new footwear? That's fine, but if your next course of action is to bin the boxes you need to retrain yourself to put your shoes back in the box. I would guess that the amount of money spent on shoes racks and those awful hanging canvas or plastic shoe stores is astronomical. Why waste your cash when all you need to do is retain shoeboxes that can be so easily stacked? And there's usually a picture of the shoe on the box so you'll know which is which. I once saw a magazine feature recommending that you take a Polaroid of your shoes and stick it on the end of a shop-bought box so that you could identify the contents. What a waste of time when if you keep the original the job has been done for you!

If you are running out of storage space consider decluttering the room. IDEA 15, *Keep it tidy*, will guide you through the process.

Try another idea...

Tailor-made storage in the bedroom comes in many guises. Wardrobes, chests of drawers and blanket boxes all have a dedicated purpose, but each takes up an area of the floor and there is the wasted space between each item to consider (it would look ridiculous if they were rammed together side by side). Rather than buy lots of smaller pieces that are not too expensive, have you thought about investing in a larger bit of furniture, something that combines hanging and drawer space for example? The cost might be higher but in the long term it could make more efficient use of the area that it takes up.

Efficient use of space is what it boils down to, and if there is one obvious space-saving solution it is underbed storage. You don't have to buy a bed with drawers built in; why not invest in a set of drawers on castors that you can wheel in and out as required?

Side tables provide a place to put your tea in the morning but if they don't also have drawers you are again wasting a space that could provide a storage solution.

'If you can't get rid of the skeleton in your closet, you'd best teach it to dance.'
GEORGE BERNARD SHAW

Defining idea...

The primary function of the bedroom is to provide a restful and relaxing environment conducive to a restful night's sleep, so keep your bedroom clutter-free. Well-planned storage is the solution.

Q **My bedroom is pretty tiny and while I appreciate the benefits of a built-in wardrobe, I just feel that dedicating a whole wall to this would make it feel much smaller. Is there an alternative?**

A *Think back to the key issue, which is efficient use of space. By moving your bed around would it give you access to any alcoves or recesses in your bedroom? Are they deep enough to take the width of a hanger? It's quite simple to fix a pole across the space but if you think about it why have just one? If you consider the length of shirts and jackets you could easily fit in two poles, thus doubling your storage. A blind is a much more contemporary way to cover up these areas, though curtains could be better suited to the style of your room. Could you have cupboards built around the door? The space above the door is often left bare but it could provide storage for items that you don't need on a regular basis.*

Q **If I do decide to have built-in cupboards, what will I gain?**

A *The benefits of floor-to-ceiling wardrobes built to accommodate any recesses or angles in your room is that you can design the space to provide storage for all your clothes and shoes and bed linen. If you include some wire trays or baskets on runners, you will also have somewhere for underwear and even toiletries.*

43

The best-dressed floors are wearing...

Rugs come in a range of classic and contemporary designs. Are you familiar with the feeling that comes when you arrive somewhere and wish you'd made a bit more effort with your outfit? If you leave all of your floors without rugs you are condemning them to a similar fate.

Even the finest carpet or most expensive stone floor will look a million dollars when it's dressed up with a rug.

What do they bring to a room? Sometimes colour, sometimes a change of texture, sometimes they are there to define a particular space. But the beauty of rugs is their versatility.

Imagine a room in summer with a lovely stripped wooden floor. The sun is pouring through the windows and the light colour of the room is perfect for the season. Go on and picture the scene in winter when the floor seems to be draughty and the cool colours send a chill through your heart. Now introduce a lovely, thick rug into the room, something with lots of texture which will contrast beautifully with the smooth wood, in a warm colour that draws you in to the space. It's a quick and easy way of adapting a room through the seasons.

Here's an idea for you...

If you've already designed and decorated your home, you can commission a rug to work with a particular colour scheme or style of interior. There are skilled crafts people who will endeavour to work to a brief. You can contact them through local art galleries or by searching on the web. Have a clear idea of how much you wish to spend, but more importantly a definite picture in your mind of the colours and patterns that you would like to include. Make sure that whoever you work with has seen the room.

They may be just a finishing touch, but what a finish they deliver.

Aside from the comfort issue what else do they bring? They can be used to delineate different areas of the room. If you have a dining area at the end of the lounge, putting a rug down in that space creates the visual illusion of a different area. If you have an enormous lounge or live in a studio-style space with no dividing walls, use a rug to mark out different territories. Place one in the middle of a group of chairs and a sofa and it draws everyone into that space. Put one down in between the kitchen and the seating area and it breaks up that part of the room and emphasises the fact that there are two distinct zones in use.

The successful positioning of rugs relies on drawing the eye to a particular space. This might suggest that the rug needs to be brightly coloured or boldly patterned, but that isn't the case. The mere fact that it sits proud of the floor beneath is enough to work its magic. You can use a pale-coloured rug on top of a natural wood floor and still achieve your aim, but if it has a border in a contrasting colour that may help.

Anyone who is well travelled will have tales of bargaining with a rug dealer somewhere in the world. It almost seems to be a right of passage. Whether you buy an authentic oriental rug, a kelim or a dhurrie, one of the best things about purchasing these pieces is that you have something with a memory attached, but also something that is actually useful. Amazingly, these ethnic items will suit a wide range of interiors. Somehow the woven patterns, stylized motifs and knotted construction of these different rugs blend and complement everywhere from traditional cluttered country cottage to a modern, minimalist, loft-style interior.

I seem to have dwelt on one particular style and should now say that many modern designs are considered works of art. They are so gorgeous that you will consider hanging them from your walls (which is easily done with good strong carpet grippers by the way). Companies commission designers to produce rugs that reflect their personal style and it is not just interior specialists that they choose. The cross-over between fashion and furnishings is nowhere more evident than in rugs. Paul Smith may have designed the perfect suit and diversified into glasses, bags and shoes but you can now also walk all over one of his striped rugs.

See IDEA 39, *The essential extras,* for other ideas on how to accessorise a space.

Try another idea...

'*To me a lush carpet of pine needles or spongy grass is more welcome than the most luxurious Persian rug.*'
HELEN KELLER

Defining idea...

If you have any lingering doubts about rugs, then consider the following scenarios:

- You have a wood floor in the lounge, all the seats are taken but you would like some people to be able to sit on the floor: a thick rug provides some cushioning for their bottoms.

- The colour scheme in your bedroom is fairly neutral but you are aware that a subtle touch of colour would add the finishing touch: a striped cotton rug, laid beside the bed, will introduce a bit of pattern to the room.

- The stone floor in the hall is very practical but it is also extremely cold: a rug placed away from the entrance but running down the rest of the room is much more inviting to new arrivals.

If you want a subtle way of adding warmth, comfort and a touch of colour or pattern to a room, you can look to rugs to provide a solution.

Defining idea...

'*A woman telling her true age is like a buyer confiding his final price to an Armenian rug dealer.*'
MIGNON McLAUGHLIN, American author and editor

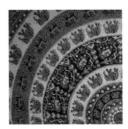 

Q   **I'm convinced that I need a rug but won't it slip all over the place on a stone floor?**

How did it go?

A   *This is a joy to answer because I am addicted to stupid gadgets and the ridiculous bits and pieces that every house should have – even if you don't know it. There are many products that will fit under rugs to keep them in place. Look for something that you can cut to fit to exactly the right size. Search for names like 'stay put' and 'non-slip' on the web and you'll find what you need.*

Q   **If I use one of these products, will it damage the rug?**

A   *It's highly unlikely. In most cases it could be really good for your rug because it will provide a barrier between the rug and the floor so protecting it from a certain amount of dirt. You'll also appreciate the fact that your rug will not be constantly moving about which makes it much easier to vacuum – essential for removing residual dust and dirt from any kind of flooring.*

 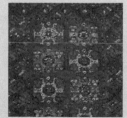

44

Take a seat

Comfort and style are essential requirements for your sofas and chairs.

Do your feet swing half-way to the floor? Does your head loll about without support when you sit down to watch the television? It probably means that you didn't put your sofa or armchair through all its paces when you went to choose it from the showroom.

The first rule of buying any piece of furniture is to sit, lie, snuggle and be a drama queen – act out all of your usual positions before you hand over the cheque. If you like to curl up in comfort, make sure your design comes with lots of throw-on cushions. The second rule is to measure it and make sure that it will get into your home.

Imagine the disappointment after waiting weeks for your custom-made sofa when it won't make it through the front door. Winch hire is an expensive business unless you are friendly with the owner of a large construction firm. You'll also have to deal with really grumpy delivery men, not a nice prospect at any time but particularly stressful when you've been camped out on the floor for weeks and are desperate to sit down in comfort.

Stick with the following guidelines when buying a chair or sofa and you can't go wrong:

- **Have some idea of the shape and style that you like.**
- **Work out your budget before you hit the shops.**
- **Be sure of the space that you have allocated for your furniture.**
- **Test every seat and then test them again.**
- **Consider going direct to the manufacturer. This is a good way of saving money because you cut out the middleman, but as with buying from catalogues which could also seem a cheaper option, you have to remember that you won't get to try them out.**

The idea of the three-piece suite has a place for some people. I tend to associate it with the design of a bygone age. It is much better visually to have different pieces of furniture in a room that are tied in by colour or style but not necessarily because they are a perfect match. That way you can put a cotton-covered sofa next to a leather armchair in the lounge or a couple of armchairs in the same room as a chaise longue. I do think you are limiting yourself if you buy every seat in a matching design. Avoiding the three-piece also frees you up to spend more on a spectacular sofa, one with wonderfully luxurious feather-filled cushions and a frame which has been dowelled, screwed and glued and is constructed in hardwood. Yes it will cost a lot, but you can be sure it will last for years. You can then choose chairs that cost a little less but if upholstered in a complementary fabric and dressed up with cushions will look quite OK beside your designer sofa.

When you are investing in these pieces of furniture you should also bear in mind that you may well decide to redecorate and change the colour scheme in your room long before they are worn out. Now it is possible that if you have a small armchair upholstered in blue, which was one of the colours of the scheme that you were working with when you brought it, you could afford to have it reupholstered when you decide to opt for an all-white room. However, with a red sofa that no longer works with the room, you are looking at a much larger investment to replace the covers. I'm not saying that you should always choose neutral colours for sofas and chairs, because that would be very boring indeed. But what I am suggesting is that you have in mind future options. Loose covers might be worth considering, for example. Sometimes you can get two sets for the price of one in summer sales and that opens up your options considerably. For this same reason, unless you are wealthy enough to change sofas and chairs every few years, it's a good idea to avoid high-fashion or gimmicky designs that will look dated quickly.

> '*A chair is a very difficult object. A skyscraper is almost easier. That is why Chippendale is famous.*'
> LUDWIG MIES VAN DER ROHE

Defining idea...

Take a look at **IDEA 50**, *The pattern rules*, **for some thoughts on choice of fabrics.**

Try another idea...

Antiques and collectable pieces really sit outside of this framework. The sheer diversity in chair design can be quite bewildering, and these are pieces of furniture that become collectable items much more quickly than sofas.

Of course there are the historical designs. A classic Charles Rennie Mackintosh curved wooden armchair or an upholstered Bauhaus design by Walter Groupius, for example, would both be happy additions to any expert's chair collection. But if you aren't looking for investments and just want somewhere comfortable to sit, then one or two different armchairs from a high-street department store are just what you need.

> '*The discontented man finds no easy chair.*'
> BENJAMIN FRANKLIN

Defining idea...

Whatever style of furniture you choose, make sure it fulfils the most important criteria of all: comfort.

How did it go?

Q   I am thinking about buying a second-hand sofa to save money. Is this a good idea?

A   *Sadly, what you save on the initial purchase you may have to spend on restoration. Restoring an old sofa is a skilled task. The piece may have to be stripped back all the way to the frame. Then it's possible any rotten elements will need to be replaced and, of course, it will need restuffing. Also you have to figure in the cost of new fabric which, depending on the size of the piece, could prove very costly indeed.*

Q   What if I wanted to invest in an antique?

A   *Make sure that you examine any piece carefully. If the legs, for example, look a different colour to the wood on the back of a sofa or chair, it could mean that they are replacements rather than originals. Look at all the different parts of the piece – there will be fabric, wood and metal components and if each one needs repairing it will add to the cost. You might want to consider restoration, where a craftsperson will try to return it as close as possible to its original state. Or you could consider conservation, where repairs will be made but the priority is to preserve the integrity of the furniture, so that work is kept to a minimum.*

45

A taste for tiles

Dress up your walls with pattern and colour – oh, and tiles are practical too. If you are considering how to treat the walls in your bathroom, kitchen or hallway, you could do a lot worse than to tile them.

The hardwearing quality of tiles is enough to recommend them for any hardworking area. Resistant to dirt and easy to clean, they make a logical choice for rooms that receive a lot of wear and tear.

If you think about the volume of water that gets splashed around in the bathroom, the amount of steam in the kitchen, and the rain and dirt that flies around in a hallway, it becomes obvious why tiles are a good choice for the walls.

So how do you choose your tiles? Some of the things you need to consider are common to all of the areas above; others may be more specific to a particular room. You are going to be influenced by the colour, pattern and texture of a tile. If you have already decided on the scheme for your room, then are you going to match the colour of the paint on your walls with a slightly lighter or darker shade or do you want to pick a completely contrasting colour? Are you interested in creating a

Here's an idea for you...

Don't just place tiles on your walls – you can use them to dress up window sills too. If you have a deep enough sill, then cover it with colourful designs to add interest to what is frequently a bare and undecorated part of the home. They can be used to add a quirky touch where the window treatment that has been used is quite plain. And they are hardwearing too. You won't need to change them as often as you would need to repaint the surface.

...and another...

If you have lots of tiles left over from tiling the kitchen, think about using them to cover the top of a table – it's a neat way of dressing up a junk shop buy.

pattern or introducing a picture or mural in the room, or do you want to define two spaces with a tiled dado?

If you think about your kitchen, here are some elements that might influence your choice:

■ How much wall space are you looking to cover with the tiles? If you have wall-mounted cabinets, then you may only have a small area to tile and can afford to choose more expensive hand-made tiles over mass-produced ceramic designs.

■ Is there a space that you want to fill with a panel or mural of tiles? You could commission something from an artist but quite frankly there are a huge variety of designs that can be bought off the shelf. You'll find trees, fruit, plants, flowers and animals to name a few. These can be set on the wall in the middle of plain tiles or surrounded with a contrasting colour to frame the view.

■ Do you want to combine mostly plain tiles with just a scattering of patterned ones? A few hand-painted delft tiles might look perfect introduced at random in a rustic country kitchen, while metallic abstract designs could be a way to add an intriguing detail in a modern room. In the bathroom you are likely to be covering large areas so cost is much more of a consideration. I would recommend that you budget to cover the largest area possible. It makes cleaning and maintaining the bathroom so much more easy if virtually all the walls are tiled.

For other ideas on covering walls, see IDEA 46, *It's in the papers.*

Try another idea...

- Do you have a separate shower area that needs completely tiling? If that cuts into your budget, then limit yourself elsewhere, for example to a tiled splashback above the sink. Stand up in your bath and tile to the height of your shoulders around that area. That should be sufficient to protect the wall from even the most vigorous of splashing bathers.

- Where you don't cover an entire wall, you may want to finish the top of these tiles with a smaller border design for the sake of neatness.

- Have you considered mosaic tiles in the bathroom? These look absolutely stunning whether they are in bright colours or natural shades. Bright Mediterranean blue mosaics have a visual impact that is unrivalled in the tile world.

Tiling the walls in your hallway may sound distinctly old-fashioned and of course this is a feature of many Victorian homes. But there is no rule that says you shouldn't use modern, cool-coloured tiles in place of the dark greens and blues that were traditionally used. Oblong-shaped designs are most definitely an option for this area.

'Decorate your home. It gives the illusion that your life is more interesting than it really is.'
CHARLES SCHULZ, cartoonist, creator of *Peanuts*

Defining idea...

How did
it go?

Q   **Once I've got my tiles up, how do I maintain them?**

A   *With a great deal of ease. A simple wipe will usually do the job, but if you are trying to remove a build-up of limescale from water splashes, use a proprietory cleaner. You will need to leave some solutions on for a few minutes but do make sure that you rinse the surface well with lots of clean water. Leaving any traces will contribute to the build-up of dirt on the surface.*

Q   **If I can't be bothered to take down some old tiles, can I just retile over the top?**

A   *This isn't ideal because of problems with sealing them at the top and bottom of any run. However, it's easy enough to tile over existing tiles as long as they are still very firmly attached to the walls. There should be no loose or cracked ones in the area. Then all you need to be concerned with is cleaning them thoroughly and removing any grease from the surface before applying the new ones over the top. Do tell your supplier that this is what you are planning so that you get the right type of adhesive for the job.*

46

It's in the papers

Back in fashion and burgeoning with design potential, wallpaper has a place in everyone's home.

I know what you are thinking. The paste pot, the collapsible table, the lining up of seams, the cutting and measuring, this is a real fag. I agree.

Save up and pay someone else to do the job. Or embrace the concept of the many new developments in wallpaper technology – it's true – and pick an easy-to-hang design. For example, wallpapers where you paste the wall and not the cut strip make the job much more approachable. You won't need masses of equipment but there are two essential tools: the paper-hanging brush, which you use to smooth over the surface and squeeze out air bubbles and excess paste, and the seam roller that ensures a flat join between two drops of paper.

Remember that you don't have to tackle an entire room. You can choose to paper just the alcoves either side of a chimneybreast, or make a feature of a single wall with the rest of the room decorated with paint. Wallpaper can hide a multitude of sins. If you use lining paper first on an uneven wall or surface with hairline cracks (check that they are not caused by any structural problems before you cover them, and that they won't get any worse) and then add the decorative paper on top, you'll

Here's an idea for you...

If you are going to use a border to create panels and frame pictures you need to make sure that the two work in harmony and don't clash. First, make sure the design of your paper complements the colour of the picture frame. Second, allow a reasonable amount of space between the edge of the frame and the border both at the sides and the top and bottom – ideally your picture should sit in the middle of your panel.

get a superb finish that paint just can't deliver. You mustn't think of wallpaper design in terms of woodchip, bubbles or garish patterns. A muted print with a sprigged flower can add a hint of pattern to a room that is so subtle as to be almost subliminal in its effect. Or a large pattern applied to just one wall will create an instant impact in the room. Retro designs can be used as the backdrop to a fifties-themed interior, while classic prints are the perfect way to complement a traditional home. Don't just limit your imagination to rolls that cover the complete wall. There are decorative friezes, borders and dados that can be used to define different areas in a room and to break up vast expanses of plain wall. For example, you can use a border design to create panels on the wall; a run of two or three across a large space gives a lovely effect and each one can frame a painting, a mirror or a print. If you have a very high ceiling, a wide border run around the room at picture rail height will help visually draw the eye down into the room. You can also use them to highlight architectural features like sloping ceilings, recesses and chimneybreasts, or run them around window and doorframes where again they will draw attention towards each particular feature of the space.

PERFECT PATTERNS

Using decorative wallpaper throughout one room will have a strong impact on the size of the space. If it's a very busy design, you can expect the room to shrink in size. One way to avoid this would be to limit your use to two or three walls and leave one area to be decorated with paint in a pale but matching colour. However, if you like the idea of creating a smaller space, go the whole way and run your design up and across the ceiling too. I have seen this done with a very pretty floral print in a bedroom and it does create a really cosy, country mood.

Another visual trick is to use stripes to run up the wall when the ceiling in the room appears to be quite low. It will instantly change the proportions of the space.

Because of the sheer diversity of designs you can use wallpaper to cheat different finishes on your walls. A leather paint effect would take some considerable time to achieve while putting up a 'faux' leather paper is a much quicker option. Covering your walls with fabric might present a considerable expense but a damask-look paper will be considerably cheaper. And there are the *trompe l'oeil* designs that are available. If you want a country scene in your living room search out a toile de Jouy design. If you'd like Doric columns in the dining room, you'll easily find a paper that you can use to cheat the look.

Have a look at IDEA 12, Decorative effects for a designer home, if you are interested in paint effects.

Try another idea…

'*Family love is messy, clinging, and of an annoying and repetitive pattern, like bad wallpaper.*'
P. J. O'ROURKE

Defining idea…

'*The whole point of camouflage is to deceive the enemy's eye, making it as difficult as possible to perceive the outline of a tank. The same is true in a papered room. For the most part, straight lines, angles and intrusive architectural lumps such as chimney breasts can be quite successfully obliterated by the pleasing distraction of pattern.*'
LAURENCE LLEWELYN-BOWEN, *BBC Good Homes Magazine*

Defining idea…

How did
it go?

Q **I've used a border to create panels around the walls in my dining room. Now I am not sure whether a picture in each one is going to look right as the pictures are different sizes but the panels are all uniform in layout.**

A *Often it's better to space the pictures out so that you have one or two empty panels in between each one that you fill. Try limiting the number of pictures that you hang rather than filling every panel.*

Q **But what about the different sizes of the pictures?**

A *Lay your pictures out. Put the biggest one down first and then try and collect together two or three others that when put in a group together equal the size of the largest. Then hang this group in a panel two or three away from the big picture.*

47

Have you wasted that loft space?

Look up to your roof if you need to expand.

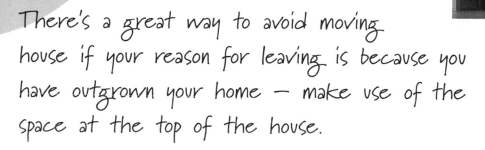

There's a great way to avoid moving house if your reason for leaving is because you have outgrown your home — make use of the space at the top of the house.

I was tiny when we had the loft converted in our family home, but I do remember that there was an awful lot of mess. Now that might be enough to put you off the idea, but if you consider the pain of packing up your house and finding somewhere else to live, then the thought of a few weeks of chaos might not seem so bad.

A loft conversion is the most sensible way of getting an extra room (well that and adding on a conservatory, but you may well have done that already).

PUT PLANS IN PLACE

First, with some basic questions...
- What is your budget?
- How will the room be used?
- Where are you going to put the extra staircase that you will need?

Here's an idea for you...

There are loft conversions and then there are loft conversions. If you have a really good budget then why not put an extra bathroom or shower space in the room? If you are worried about it taking up a lot of space, you'll find plenty of bathroom suites designed with space saving in mind. This might be the ideal space to use glass bricks as a room divider so that you are not cutting down on light in either space.

■ How are you going to lay out the space to accommodate the slopes and awkward shapes that the roof creates?

Knowing your budget is vital. That's not just what you wish to spend on the building work but also the furnishing and decoration of the room. There's no point in having all the work done if what you are then left with is plaster walls and bare floors. You need to decide on whether you are going to be putting another bed up there, if it will become an office or if it is just going to be the kids' playroom. Any of these scenarios will call on you to spend money furnishing the space.

Another reason for defining the budget is so that you can decide whether you can afford a dormer window which projects to the outside to form a full-height area in the loft with a vertical window or whether you will have to settle for a cheaper roof window which is set into the slope of the roof. Planning regulations in your area may also affect this choice.

You need to have a good idea of the ultimate use of the space because if it is going to be an office you'll need a telephone point, lots of electrical sockets for all of your computer kit, and light fittings to illuminate the work area.

See the ideas for a home office in IDEA 8, *Work that room*, for and bedroom storage in IDEA 42, *It works like a dream.*

Try another idea...

Consider up-lighters rather than a pendant fitting because they will throw light up towards what will probably be a reasonably low ceiling. If that doesn't worry you, then halogen spots set into the ceiling are a good option.

If it's going to be a spare bedroom or playroom, these things may not be of such importance to you and you may be able to save money by not including all of the above.

'The sky's the limit if you have a roof over your head.'
SOL HUROK, Russian-born impresario

Defining idea...

If you are converting a loft space for teenagers, then soundproofing has to be a priority and that may up the costs. Depending on the size of the space you may want to add a false wall inside the structure. Use timber battens to support a layer of plasterboard around the room. Think about where the TV and stereo are going to be placed. For starters make sure that the TV is not positioned against a party wall. Music can be muffled by hanging the speakers instead of standing them on a solid surface, or by positioning them on foam.

'Men of lofty genius when they are doing the least work are most active.'
LEONARDO DA VINCI

The reason for deciding on the position of the staircase is because you are going to have to lose space from somewhere on the floor below. If you are worried about it encroaching on a bedroom, then maybe think about a spiral staircase. As long as the children who may be using this are not too young it can be a space-saving solution. Another option, if the builders can work it in, is to make the flight quite steep. Use open treads to allow light into the area.

EXTRA TOUCHES

If you can afford it, think about including built-in storage in the room. It will work around the slopes of the ceiling making the maximum use of any awkward areas in the room. Because the room that the conversion creates is unlikely to be huge, you want to avoid cluttering it up with lots of different pieces of freestanding furniture wherever possible.

Also, consider what type of heating to put in the roof (and make sure it is well insulated whatever you choose). Check with your builder whether it is possible to include underfloor heating – this is by far the best solution because you won't have to worry about losing wall space to radiators.

Careful planning is the key to a successful conversion, so take time to get everything right.

Q **Do I need to get any approval for the job?**

*How did
it go?*

A *There is no doubt that you will need to check with your local authority or
council before getting on with the job, and your builder should know which
local officials you need to speak to. If you employ an architect they may
take on the job of getting approval for your conversion. You will also have
to comply with local fire regulations at every point in the construction of
your loft. Some properties may not require planning permission, provided
the loft conversion is the first extension to the house and it doesn't exceed
a certain size.*

Q **If I do go through with this, is it true that it will add value to my
property?**

A *If the job is done properly a loft conversion will increase the value of your
house considerably. Make sure that you have done everything legally
required for the work as a future buyer's surveyor will check on the
permissions for the conversion, and its compliance with the relevant
regulations.*

48

A night on the tiles

A fantastic range of looks are made possible with tiled floors. You can lay down all sorts of patterns and even include pictures when you put down a tiled floor.

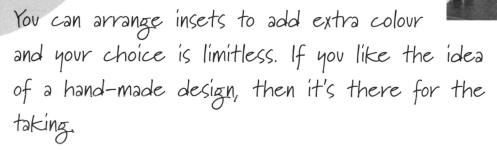

You can arrange insets to add extra colour and your choice is limitless. If you like the idea of a hand-made design, then it's there for the taking.

If you require a reclaimed floor to fit in with a renovated building, it's just a quick tour of France, Spain or Italy away. Well actually no, someone will have imported it for you, but those are three of the countries from where they are sourced.

The finish on tiles varies enormously. There are matt, unglazed surfaces, high gloss finishes and various sheens caused by the application of different glazes. If you love a particular look, then make sure before you buy your tiles that the finish will not be affected in the sealing process, as some tiles are pre-sealed before they are sold while others are sealed once they have been laid.

There's no question that tiles are hardwearing. But anyone who's walked across a stone-cold floor in the middle of the night might be wondering whether a carpet

Here's an idea for you...

When you are deciding on which colour of tile to choose, consider how they will work with other elements in the room. If you're planning to put down some rugs, will they complement the colours in the weave? If you have already bought curtains or blinds for the windows, will the tiles pick up on a colour in the print or design of the fabric that you have chosen?

would offer more comfort. If you can afford it, the best solution to that problem is to install underfloor heating.

The sheer variety of tiles on offer might be a little confusing so let's address a few specifics. For a rustic touch with a grand history turn to terracotta. Colours may vary. You'll find yellow and ochre tiles from Tuscany and rich red designs from Mexico, but one quality that most share is the rough and ready finish to these tiles. Don't be surprised to find slight pitting and areas that have been eroded in the surface of the tiles. You are getting a product that looks like it has lived a little, even if it was only recently manufactured. This of course makes it ideal for areas of heavy traffic where there is nothing better than a surface that doesn't show the dirt. But it also means that if you want the colour of terracotta but with a smoother finish you need to search out very specific extruded designs. These are sometimes confused with quarry tiles but in fact the two are made from different clays. The manufacturing process means that quarry tiles are much harder then terracotta and also less porous.

Ceramic tiles are the first choice for most bathrooms, most kitchens and a mix of other spaces where you want to add colour and pattern to the floor. Because they are made in moulds, they offer a uniformity that makes them easy to work with. Not only can you guarantee straight lines, but they are also simple to cut so can be worked into all sorts of nooks and crannies, curving around pedestals and butting up against waste pipes without too much difficulty. Just a point to bear in mind: if you know that some tiles will need to be cut you should allow for extra when you measure up and order them. If you break some, then go back a week later to the shop for a few extras, these may come from a different batch and you won't be able to guarantee an exact colour match.

For information on wall tiles, see IDEA 45, *A taste for tiles.*

Try another idea...

Mosaic tiles can be used to stunning effect. Use different colours to create borders in a room, or lay an oblong in a contrasting colour in the middle of the floor or beside the bath to create the illusion of a mat. The different types, including ceramic, marble and stone, can be combined in a floor but it really is best to stick with one type for a uniform finish. You can be as adventurous as you want in creating patterns but you'll need a very patient fitter for a highly detailed design. In fact you are probably better employing the services of a mosaic artist if you are looking for something very decorative.

'**Scrubbing floors and emptying bedpans has as much dignity as the Presidency.**'
RICHARD M. NIXON

Defining idea...

Part of the attraction of a mosaic floor is the contrast in texture between the tiles themselves and the grouting that holds them in place. This gives a pleasing, slightly rough feeling underfoot which also helps to make it less slippery than a floor covered in larger tiles. That's one of the biggest benefits of choosing it for the bathroom.

Bear in mind when buying mosaics sold by the sheet that the colour and tone of the stones may vary across each sheet. Make sure that if there is a mix of pink and brown tints in the mosaic, for example, that you don't end up with 80 per cent brown sheets and 20 per cent pink. You want to be able to have an even mix across the room, which is pleasing to the eye.

'**The finest workers in stone are not copper or steel tools, but the gentle touches of air and water working at their leisure with a liberal allowance of time.**'
HENRY DAVID THOREAU

Defining idea...

How did it go?

Q   I've put down unglazed floor tiles and I am aware that these need to be sealed. Are there any particular things to bear in mind?

A   *You must be sure that the tiles are completely dry. If you seal them and any are damp you may well ruin them. Also make sure that the room is clean and free of dust or you will be sealing that into the surface too. You may need to test an area to see how porous the surface is: you don't want to use too much or too little sealant and it could be that your tiles will require two or three light coats in preference to one heavy one. If sealant is pooling on the surface you are applying too much.*

Q   And when should I grout them?

A   *With unglazed tiles you want to apply a seal first, allow that to dry, then grout and then seal again. You really do need to make sure that the surface is dry before you apply the grout and also that the gaps between the tiles are free of any dirt or debris. There are various different types of grout so check with your supplier which type would be best for your tiles.*

49

An organised mind

Nothing in the world beats brilliant storage. If you think that makes me sound rather sad and probably a compulsive obsessive, you may be right. I can't imagine how I would live without good storage in every room in my house.

I am not someone who can bear to be encircled by mess. Without being too dull about it, my view is that if you live surrounded by clutter, you will always feel slightly disorganized about your life.

Please don't turn the page if you think this is insanity. Just try a bit of organisation in your home and see how pleased you are with the results.

In most rooms in the house, built-in cupboards are worth their weight in gold. Now here I would suggest that you don't attempt a quick DIY job – find a craftsperson and pay them good money to put in cupboards that fit any wasted space. Obvious places to consider are at either side of a chimneybreast, in a recess caused by the juxtaposition of two rooms and under the stairs. If you aren't in a position to fund that kind of work, then go out and get a second job. Sorry, that's harsh. It's just that when you see a room with storage that has been built to perfectly fit a particular space, then other options often come a poor second.

Here's an idea for you...

Try and store all of the electrical items in your living room in one or two dedicated units. There is nothing more unsightly than the spaghetti mess of cables from a video and TV, which are just put on tables or on stands. A unit that houses these two items will keep all of the electrical wiring together even if it's just a trolley. Also be logical – try and store CDs in a unit with the player, and the same for DVDs.

BREAK IT DOWN

The key to good storage is to consider the room first and the storage second. Don't just go out and buy a cupboard that you think might 'fit in somewhere'. You want to be clear about the room it will work in, the purpose it will serve, and whether it is going to offer the maximum possible storage space for the room. My advice is to approach it on a room-by-room basis, as your requirements for the lounge are very different to your needs in the study. Apply a critical eye to each room, breaking down your possessions into groups. Which items need to be within easy and accessible reach? Are there certain things, which only get occasional use? Most importantly, is there anything that you can get rid of? Also apply a bit of lateral thinking. Not all storage has to be positioned on the floor and sometimes the best solutions are concealed from the eye.

I know from personal experience that the more space I have, the more I fill. And the longer I live somewhere, the more clutter I accumulate. What this means in practical terms it that your storage needs may well change over time, but start with the best of basics.

Concealed storage has real appeal. It could be a table that has drawers hidden underneath or it could be a footstool with space beneath when you lift the lid. The more items like this that you can find, the less you will need to rely on cupboards that take up valuable floor space. Of course there are some items that you want to see and have easy access to, like books. Consider if there are any wasted spaces in the house where you might put a bookshelf – the landing is often an area that is left clear of any furniture but if you think about it, might there be room for a full-height set of bookshelves?

Before you embark on your storage voyage, it's worth spending time decluttering your home, IDEA 15, *Keep it tidy*, has some great hints.

Try another idea...

Every hall should have somewhere to deposit coats and shoes (umbrellas, school bags and gym kits too). Look for a unit that has a mirror at the front and shelves concealed behind. These are widely available from stores like Ikea. Failing that, think about putting a chest or settle in the hall which has storage space beneath the seat.

The bathroom can be a real challenge if you have a fairly small room. There are units available that fit over the top of the toilet providing shelves or a cabinet above your head for keeping all your necessary bits and pieces. And that is a good example of clever use of space, which is what good storage is all about. A large, mirrored and lit bathroom cabinet can be pricey, but what you lose in the initial outlay you will gain over time from having a dedicated space in which to put toiletries.

'Search the true order Blunted by wind-blown thoughts. And to every Fall-hurled leaf a place.'
LEO TIFAL, Canadian poet

Defining idea...

Now the office is a challenge, but I would recommend that you invest in a filing cabinet and buy a desk that has plenty of drawers. Or, look out for old shop fittings – units with stacks and stacks of drawers or industrial shelving with plenty of open racks for slotting in baskets.

The secret of good storage is adaptability and versatility, so spend time researching dual-purpose pieces and practical items that fulfil all of your needs.

Q I can deal with all the large objects in my home but what about the little things that litter each room?

A *I suspect this is a problem for many people. Where do you put magazines in the lounge? How do you store the washing-up brush and scrubber in the kitchen? What do you do with the pens and pencils in your office? These are all small scale but they need a home just as much as larger things. Often these types of items are really dull so try and be decorative with the storage. A neat little jug is ideal for the kitchen ephemera, a kilner jar perfect for pens in the office, and I would recommend a purpose-built rack for your magazines but consider a wall-mounted one that won't clutter up the floor.*

Q Sounds very bitty – isn't that what I'm trying to avoid?

A *Yes, it may be, but unless you are going to put absolutely everything away behind closed doors (and yes, I would love to recommend you live like that), then you do have to have certain items out on the table top or sink surface and within easy reach. That's why I recommend that you try to choose decorative items for the storage.*

50

The pattern rules

Here's how different motifs can work to the good of your home. Of all the things that can upset the eye when you walk into a room, an excessive use of patterns must be one of the most common.

It's a visual nightmare when there are so many different things going on in a space that your eye has no idea on which to focus.

That's not to say that there is any reason why you shouldn't employ different patterns in the same room, but there is a way of using them to their best advantage. The rulebook that says you cannot combine paisleys with stripes or checks with florals has not been written – and quite rightly. Using patterns is a great way of brightening a colour scheme and adding visual excitement and interest to a space, but it just needs handling with some care to make any combination work to its best advantage.

Whether they are on patterned fabric or accessories, patterns can be used to make a statement about the style of the room and emphasise its personality.

Tartan, for example, immediately makes a room feel warm and cosy – amazing really when you consider that Scotland is hardly the warmest place on the planet. I suspect that it is more to do with the association with cosy fires and highland hunting lodges. It can be used to add a quirky touch to townhouses.

Here's an idea for you...

When you are making up items from lengths of fabric be aware that a very busy design should be used with care. If the fabric has a hectic pattern, keep the item it is being made up into quite simple, for example if you are making up a highly decorative material into a bedspread, avoid frills and flounces to trim your design.

Simple floral patterns suggest spring. They are the optimists in the fabric family symptomatic of new starts and fresh beginnings. Walk into a room where these designs have been used and even the most dedicated of minimalists will enjoy a lift to their spirits. Choose florals for a conservatory or south-facing lounge.

Stripes have the effect of making a space seem quite 'grown up'. There is something about the regular nature of this pattern that makes people sit with straight backs and sip their tea without slopping it into the saucer. It has a formal quality to it that can be usefully employed in period houses.

Geometrics could be seen as the juveniles in the group. From squares and circles to lines and squiggly shapes, these patterns evoke a mood of careless enjoyment. Slightly cheeky and reminiscent of the 50s, 60s and 70s when women were liberated and music became rock and roll, they are perfect for modern flats and new conversions.

Now that is just a few examples of the designs you can work with. There are hundreds of other options from classical scenes to animal prints and oriental flowers to ethnic motifs, each one evoking a different mood.

So how do you combine them in a space? It used to be the norm that you would use the largest motif on the biggest available surface, so huge flowers would end up on the curtains and you would graduate patterns down according to the scale of the area that they would cover. Medium sprigs would be used to upholster sofas and small buds spent their days covering cushions. There is a better way. Start with a decorative pattern, be it a fabric, wallpaper or even a carpet. Next find a plain design that works with that pattern – it might be paint for the walls or a fabric to upholster a chair – and finally choose a smaller scale pattern in the same colourway to complete the trio. If it's a fabric this will be used to cover cushions but it could just as easily be a patterned throw that will go over the back of a sofa.

For more information on different types of fabrics, see IDEA 36, *Softly, softly.*

Try another idea...

Here are a few ideas to help you work with pattern...

- Avoid using lots of tiny motifs in the same space – it will look much too busy.

'When patterns are broken, new worlds emerge.'
TULI KUPFERBERG, musician

Defining idea...

- Think about using large designs with care: if the motif on a wallpaper is very big, how many complete designs will fit in to the drop on the wall? If you can only see one or two, is it going to work?

- Where your walls are plain, introduce patterns on cushion covers or lampshades. If your furniture is all relatively plain, use a patterned paint effect or wallpaper on the walls.

- Don't mix two very different styles – avoid teaming Chinese-influenced oriental designs and an African-style ethnic pattern in the same room, for example.

'A designer knows he has achieved perfection not when there is nothing left to add, but when there is nothing left to take away.'
ANTOINE DE SAINT-EXUPÉRY

Defining idea...

Make your colour choices with care when you mix up different patterns and you can create quite spectacular effects in a room.

How did
it go?

Q **I have never tried combining designs before. What patterns do you suggest I use?**

A *Some of the best pairings of patterns team stripes with checks or with florals. These are really simple to make work together. If you imagine a blue gingham tablecloth and dining chairs with loose covers made from ticking you should be able to visualise what I mean. In the same way, picture a red chintzy sofa sitting in front of a wall papered with a pencil thin red stripe design.*

Q **So what about the colour choices?**

A *Keep the colours of your patterns as close to each other as possible. That way you are less likely to make any mistakes. It can help to put together a colour scheme if you start with a patterned fabric as your inspiration. This makes it easy to choose a colour for the carpet, because you can choose the same shade as the background of the fabric for the floor. And you can pick out one of the colours from the patterned design to use as the choice of paint for the walls.*

51

Wood looks

From bare boards to the finest finishes, choose wood for your floors.

There is something very appealing about walking into a room with bare boards. It has a pared down simplicity that can make other more exotic options seem a little extravagant.

Plain old oak boards allowed to gain the patina of old age, or pine bleached or limed to give a white finish have a simple appeal.

Now that is the most basic type, but when you add parquet, wood laminates, new beech and hardwood flooring, maple, walnut, ash, birch and cherry into the mix you get some idea of the rich variety of looks that are available to you if you opt for wood.

Wood works in every setting, from the oldest rustic cottage to the most loft-style apartment, and that is a great part of its appeal. It is cooler than carpet but much warmer than stone, makes the perfect background for rugs and will work with virtually any colour scheme. In fact if you can decide on nothing other than a wooden floor as part of your decorating scheme for a room, then at least you can be assured that you have made an excellent first step in the planning process.

Use paints or stains to achieve a mock-tiled appearance or a chequerboard effect. Painting alternate floorboards in two different colours can look stunning used across a large area. For the more adventurous why not choose an area, say in front of the fireplace, and add a *trompe l'oeil* rug?

Prices vary enormously, from very cheap products that you can lay yourself to top-of-the-range materials that call for a professional fitter. If you are lucky enough to have inherited a wood floor in your home, do think very carefully before you decide to cover it up with another flooring product as you may be wasting money and time.

AGE OLD

Old wood floors should be kept where possible. Sanding, stripping and finishing is within most people's range of expertise even if these jobs are time consuming and very messy. If you have just plain boards, then it is quite straightforward, however if you discover that you have parquet you need to approach it with a little more care. Any loose blocks, for example, should be refitted before you make any attempt to renovate the actual surface of the wood.

I have mentioned liming already. This relatively simple process should be employed when you have dark boards and you want to lighten the mood in the room. All you need to do is clean the surface and remove any varnish, then rub either watered-down white paint or a proprietary product into the floor. It really is that simple.

'My idea of superwoman is someone who scrubs her own floors.'
BETTE MIDLER

Should you wish to darken the wood, the range of stains, varnishes and waxes available to you will allow you to pick the perfect shade for your floor.

MODERN CHOICES

Consider the following, which are two of the
most popular choices for a wood floor:

If you want to consider adding
rugs in the room, see IDEA 43,
*The best-dressed floors are
wearing...*

*Try
another
idea...*

- Veneered or laminate flooring can be pre-assembled in long strips ready to clip
  together. It comes in several different grades and is impact- and scratch-resistant.

- Hardwood floor can come in either square-edge or tongue-and-groove planks
  and can be supplied to you either finished. It also comes in a range of different
  patterns, including maple, ash, cherry, oak and beech.

If you want a new wood floor, then for the ultimate in durability choose a solid
hardwood floor: it'll gain character with age and will last you for decades. Because
you are going to live with it for years, and it won't be cheap, start out right and get
it fitted by a professional. This type of flooring is at the top of the price range. For
less expensive options consider laminate strips, many of which can be laid by even
an incompetent DIYer. Bear in mind that laminate flooring may have only the
thinnest of veneers on top of the wood facing and it won't be as durable as some of
the more expensive options.

Wood doesn't need much maintenance. Regular vacuuming will keep down the
level of dust in the room if you have old floorboards or just use a broom to sweep
up when you feel the need. New products will benefit from a light mopping – make
sure that you are not soaking the floor and you may want to wax them from time to
time, but as long as they have been properly sealed in the first place they are
relatively maintenance-free. If an area is in bright sunlight you can get some
discoloration over time, so it may be sensible to move furniture around occasionally
and place rugs in different parts of the room according to the seasons.

How did
it go?

Q   **If I choose wood instead of carpet, how long can I expect my floor to last?**

A   *Solid hardwood flooring will be around long after your grandchildren have walked across it for the last time, if properly looked after, kept dry and protected with polish. Laminate flooring will last anything from 10–20 years and good fitting is key to prolonging its life.*

Q   **You have mentioned mopping and sweeping, but what if I get a scuffmark on the floor?**

A   *Dirty marks should be ideally cleaned up immediately before they have time to dry. The best approach is to use a sponge which you have dampened with a solution of very dilute washing-up liquid and warm water. Do not use too much water as it might cause surface discoloration. Do remember that gravel and dirt are the main enemies and, if worked into your floor, will stain and scratch the surface. Use a heavy-duty mat both inside and outside the front and back doors. Avoid dragging heavy items across the floor as they might gouge it.*

Inspiration for your home

Straight-talking advice about planning and completing your interiors.

Sometimes it's almost impossible to see the wood for the trees. However much you try to focus on one particular aspect of design, it is all too easy to get bogged down with all the details.

It's all very well for trained interior designers to tackle a room, but what about us mere mortals who approach the task with a little fear and considerable trepidation?

There are so many sources of inspiration for colour schemes that just deciding on the theme can take some considerable time. But once you have taken that first tentative step, what are your priorities?

Planning is the key. You want to arrange an order of work for the room so that each task fits in logically with the next. Make a checklist of all the jobs that will need to done, allocate each an estimated time from start to finish, and then work out how you are going to co-ordinate all the different tasks.

Here's an idea for you... **When you are working out the budget for your room, always leave a float outside of the overall budget. There is always an extra cost that comes up and you don't want to have to find money that you haven't got. Make sure that you've got a detailed quotation from everyone involved in the job; costs can sometimes mysteriously escalate if you don't keep an eye on your purse.**

Any structural changes have to be completed first. If the chimneybreast is coming out or you are removing a wall, get these jobs out of the way before you proceed any further. This would be the right time to get any rewiring done, or to sort out additional lights and sockets. Just think a little bit ahead if you can bear it. Would it also be worth having cabling for your house alarm or the wires for wall-mounted speakers for the stereo system sunk into the wall? If you are going to have to replaster, then you may as well get everything done in one fell swoop.

Next, make a decision on your flooring and get the order in. If the supplier is not going to lay the floor, then you need to marry up the arrival of the flooring with a fitter. I would add a note of caution here: certain types of flooring need to acclimatise to the room in which they will be laid, so you may need to allow a period of time between the delivery of the flooring and the date that you book the fitter. It's much easier to bring fitters into a reasonably empty room than to have to shift out all the furniture or have them move it around while they work. It will cut down on stress levels if you can get the flooring in place before anything else that you have ordered arrives.

If you are going to have pieces of furniture upholstered in a specific fabric rather than buy them off the shop floor, then find out how long the job will take. You don't want to be left with a completed room and then have to sit on boxes for three weeks. Once you have worked out delivery dates (and try and get all the furniture delivered within a few days of each other) you can arrange to decorate the room.

If you are going to use decorators make it very clear that you have a start and finish date in mind. All too often I hear of situations where the job is half finished but then workmen are called off to another site which is allegedly more pressing. It may be to someone else but it most certainly isn't to you. I can't stress enough how important it is that you make this clear. It causes so many problems when you have to try and drag people back to finish a job. It's much more relaxing for you to watch decorators work in a room without the finished floor, and it is much easier if you are doing the work yourself to function in a space where you are not worried about drips of paint or blobs of paste marking a new carpet – so ideally you should get this out of the way before the floor goes down.

Unless you are buying ready-made curtains or blinds you need to be aware of how long it will take for these items to be made up. And also be sure that they can be hung after all the decorating is completed. Painting window frames is much more straightforward when there is no fabric hanging in the way. Once you have chosen all the elements for your room and decided on which professionals you are going to use, do impress on them the importance of your own schedule. That way there can be no misunderstandings further down the line.

With the plans in place you should be able to relax and enjoy it as your scheme slowly comes together.

If you are having difficulties planning your room, see IDEA 2, *You've got the look*, for ideas on setting styles.

Try another idea...

'*Interior design is a travesty of the architectural process and a frightening condemnation of the credulity, helplessness and gullibility of the most formidable consumers – the rich.*'
STEPHEN BAYLEY, design critic

Defining idea...

'*Always design a thing by considering it in its next larger context – a chair in a room, a room in a house, a house in an environment, an environment in a city plan.*'
ELIEL SAARINEN, architect and designer

Defining idea...

How did
it go?

Q **I've made a list and created a rough plan of the timing but I am struggling to co-ordinate all the different aspects of the job. How do I go about it?**

A *It can seem like a monumental juggling act but I would suggest that you take each element and give it a priority so that the larger jobs are completed first and any small finishing touches dealt with at the end. Don't underestimate the importance of this part of the job. It may drive you to distraction but it is the most valuable thing that you can do.*

Q **What do I do if the decorators fall behind schedule?**

A *Unfortunately this can have a knock-on effect so it may be worth you warning people further down the line in advance of any delay. If this is going to cause too many more problems with your original plans, then consider revising the schedule of works involved.*

The end...

Or is it a new beginning? We hope that this book has inspired you to redecorate a room, change the layout of a space or clear the clutter from your home to make it a relaxing and enjoyable place to live. When visitors walk through the door, we hope you knock them sideways with your inspirational use of colour and clever design tricks in every room. Let us know if that's the case. We'd like to be amazed and impressed in just the same way as your houseguests.

So why not let us know about it? Tell us how you got on. What did it for you – what helped you create your ideal living space? Maybe you've got some tips of your own you want to share (see next page). If you liked this book you may find we have more brilliant ideas that could help change your life for the better.

If there is another aspect of your life that you want to work on, whether it relates to your fluctuating finances, your desire to lose weight and get fit, or even how you relate to your kids, you'll find lots more informative guides online at www.infideas.com

You can contact us via this website, or if you prefer to write then send your letters to: *Create Your Dream Home,* The Infinite Ideas Company Ltd, Belsyre Court, 57 Woodstock Road, Oxford OX2 6JH, United Kingdom.

We want to know what you think, because we're all working on making our lives better too. Give us your feedback and you could win a copy of another *52 Brilliant Ideas* book of your choice. Or maybe get a crack at writing your own.

Good luck. Be brilliant.

Offer one

CASH IN YOUR IDEAS

We hope you enjoy this book. We hope it inspires, amuses, educates and entertains you. But we don't assume that you're a novice, or that this is the first book that you've bought on the subject. You've got ideas of your own. Maybe our author has missed an idea that you use successfully. If so, why not send it to info@infideas.com, and if we like it we'll post it on our bulletin board. Better still, if your idea makes it into print we'll send you £50 and you'll be fully credited so that everyone knows you've had another Brilliant Idea.

Offer two

HOW COULD YOU REFUSE?

Amazing discounts on bulk quantities of Infinite Ideas books are available to corporations, professional associations and other organizations.

For details call us on:
+44 (0)1865 292045
fax: +44 (0)1865 292001
or e-mail: info@infideas.com

Where it's at...